JUDAISM
AND
SPIRITUAL
ETHICS

NILES E. GOLDSTEIN
and
STEVEN S. MASON

Foreword by
EUGENE B. BOROWITZ

UAHC PRESS
NEW YORK, NEW YORK

Library of Congress Cataloging-in-Publication Data

Goldstein, Niles Elliott, 1966-
    Judaism and spiritual ethics / Niles E. Goldstein and Steven S.
Mason ; foreword by Eugene B. Borowitz
    p.   cm.
    Includes selections from Ma'alot ha-midot in Hebrew, with
English translation.
    Includes bibliographical references.
    ISBN 0-8074-0601-5 (pbk. : alk. paper)
    1. Anav, Jehiel ben Jekuthiel ben Benjamin, 13th cent. Ma'alot
ha-midot. 2. Ethics, Jewish. I. Mason, Steven S. II. Borowitz,
Eugene B. III. Anav, Jehiel ben Jekuthiel ben Benjamin, 13th cent.
Ma'alot ha-midot. English & Hebrew. Selections. IV. Title.
BJ1287.G67J83 1996   96-28352
296.3'85—dc20   CIP

ACKNOWLEDGMENTS

Dr. Eugene B. Borowitz first brought to our attention the medieval Jewish values book that became the basis for this work. We thank him for this gift, as well as for the many years of teaching and guidance he has given us. We would also like to thank the following people at the UAHC Press who have worked with us on this project, both for their support and their professionalism: Annette Abramson, Stuart L. Benick, Maud Casey, David Kasakove, Azena Louis, Bennett Lovett-Graff, Ellen Nemhauser, Seymour Rossel, and Elyn Wollensky. We especially wish to thank Kathy Parnass.

In addition, both of us would like to express our gratitude to our respective congregations, which have served in their own vital ways as testing grounds for this volume. We thank the members of Temple Israel of New Rochelle, New York, and Temple Beth Am of Buffalo, New York, for their interest, concern, and opinions.

Because no discussion of Jewish spirituality makes any sense without God, we finally offer thanks to God "for our lives, which are in Your hand, for our souls, which are ever in Your keeping, for Your wondrous providence and continuous goodness, which You bestow upon us day by day." בָּרוּךְ אַתָּה יְיָ הַטּוֹב שִׁמְךָ וּלְךָ נָאֶה לְהוֹדוֹת *Baruch Atah Adonai hatov shimcha ulecha na'eh lehodot*—"Blessed is the eternal God, to whom our thanks are due."

Niles E. Goldstein
Steven S. Mason

CONTENTS

FOREWORD

Character once hardly seemed a problem for modern Jewish ethics. We took it for granted that anyone growing up in Western culture with its endless resources of human enrichment would be a fine human being. Besides, we brought to the gifts of education, democracy, and opportunity the teaching of the synagogue and the legacy of Jewish family life. Society seemed far more in need of our ethical attention than did the shaping of people into persons. And, of course, in many ways that social agenda has only expanded as the world has become our daily community.

As the twentieth century ends, our faith in the beneficent effect of our civilization seems as naive as its occurrence is understandable. Our post-ghetto/shtetl infatuation with equality simply tended to blind us to the problems it carried along with it. And these problems have multiplied over the decades since optimism was the natural mood of the liberal Jew. The preemptive messianism founded on conscience linked to political action has been tempered by a traumatizing exposure to the realities of human nature generally and the dire effects of radical individualism lured into lurid behavior. These days we do get to know and talk more about what goes on behind the personal images we construct, but while that has inured us to the omnipresence and virulence of the evil urge, it has not made its effects any less repelling.

Two major responses to the slowly dawning consciousness of our changed human situation are changing our liberal Jewish ethos. The first is the well-known turn to spirituality, the recognition that we alone are not the ground of our values and their obligations but that, in major part, spirituality lies outside us, beyond us. Euphemisms aside, God having once been proclaimed dead and agnosticism championed as the height of responsibility, we now are sufficiently postadolescent to seek a reconciliation with the Divine Parent. That may cause us difficult problems of proper symbolization and conceptualization, but they are not compelling enough to turn us away from seeking the new relationship.

The second trend concerns us here. How shall we educate for character in this upsetting time? And before we jump to our usual cop-out, "Yes, what shall we do about our children?" let it be unmistakably clear that our prime problem is adult character. Not only are we the ones who do the major damage, but if we could find ways to make nonunctuous decency a major goal of our own lives, then the single most significant influence on our children's lives would be working for their human good. It is time to remember that in its pre-American manifestations, Judaism has always primarily been a religion for adults and Jewish education has mostly been concerned with the mind and behavior of those who were mature.

Continuing that worthy pattern, we turn to the resources of our tradition for specific guidance as to what would create a worthy Jewish character. The great classics of the Jewish past, the Bible and Talmud, lavishly strew their advice throughout their pages. Not until late in the thirteenth century did a prominent Roman Jew undertake to gather and recast these counsels into twenty-four themes he thought significant for admirable living. We have no way of knowing what prompted him to do this, but it is clear that his book had a fine reception for those preprinting, medieval days. It even began a genre of Jewish writing, some of which soon became more popular than this pioneering work. Turning to it today, we are smitten with a familiar ambivalence. How foreign some of its ideas and language seem from our cyber-oriented souls! And yet, how very much like us were those Italian coreligionists of seven centuries ago, human weakness and the need to live in the Image being the constants of our nature, as Judaism sees it. Indeed, that is pretty much the way our prophets and sages have always seen it, for Yechiel has little desire to present us with a new message—one that will testify to his personal genius. Rather, he gathered a selection of biblical and talmudic materials that he knew would provide the classic guidance our spiritual geniuses set forth. Human nature is so reasonably constant that in Yechiel's pages we go back nearly two thousand years and find...ourselves. Our follies and dreams were that far back being similarly considered, as Jews then sought how they might be the selves to which experience and tradition had sensitized them—and us. We shall want to recast these old words to fit better into the knowledge and problematics of our day, but we shall in the process be refined by them and the spirituality that made them possible.

Eugene B. Borowitz
*Sigmund L. Falk Distinguished
Professor of Education and Jewish
Religious Thought*

INTRODUCTION

Sefer Ma'alot Hamidot and
Yechiel Ben Yekutiel Ben Benyamin Harofe Anav

This study of Jewish spiritual values is based on *Sefer Ma'alot Hamidot*, a thirteenth-century text by Yechiel ben Yekutiel ben Benyamin Harofe, a descendant of the Anav family of Rome. Not much is known about Yechiel's life and work other than that he was an author, a poet, and a scribe who must have gained some recognition for his *Sefer Ma'alot Hamidot*, "Book of Virtues and Values." The fact that there are more than forty extant manuscripts of this work, including a Ladino translation, indicates the popularity that *Sefer Ma'alot Hamidot* enjoyed in its time.

This book exudes great love—love of God and of Torah, as well as love for the act of teaching these values to his beloved students. *Sefer Ma'alot Hamidot* consists of twenty-four chapters or steps: *Yediat ha-El*, "Knowledge of God"; *Ahavat ha-El*, "Love of God"; *Yirat ha-Shamayim*, "Fear of God"; *Torah ve-Mitzvot*, "Teaching and Good Deeds"; *Gemilut Chasadim*, "Acts of Loving-Kindness"; *Tzedakah*, "Righteousness"; *Tefilah*, "Prayer"; *Anavah*, "Humility"; *Tzeniut*, "Modesty"; *Boshet*, "Embarrassment"; *Emunah*, "Faith"; *Temimut*, "Wholeheartedness/Integrity"; *Rachamim*, "Mercy"; *Ratzon*, "Goodwill"; *Shem Tov*, "A Good Name"; *Yetzer Tov*, "Good Inclination"; *Teshuvah*, "Repentance"; *Chochmah*, "Wisdom"; *Osher*, "Wealth"; *Zerizut*, "Diligence"; *Histapkut*, "Self-Sufficiency"; *Nidivut*, "Generosity"; *Derech Eretz*, "Courtesy"; and *Shalom*, "Peace." Yechiel often teaches these values by examining their opposites. For example, he discusses *azut*—"insolence"—in order to teach his students about *boshet*—"embarrassment"; a lesson on *shalom*—"peace"—is enriched by an examination of its opposite, *machaloket*—"controversy." Thus, by exploring opposing and decidedly negative values, Yechiel clarifies for his students the meaning and application of the positive values.

The Approach of Sefer Ma'alot Hamidot to Teaching Values

No matter where one is in the text, Yechiel urges his readers to remember at all times that the *midot* not only begin with *yediat ha-El*—"knowledge of God"—but are derived from that virtue. This is an essential point because as we progress from one virtue to the next, it becomes clear that each virtue that follows the knowledge of God also leads back to it. As a result, Yechiel's *midot* are more than just a list of virtues. They are an integrated whole whose sum is greater than its parts.

Yechiel does not approach his subject as a philosopher. Instead, he teaches each spiritual value by citing excerpts from the *Tanach* and rabbinic literature (primarily the Midrash and the Talmud). Rather than proffer a series of concepts, he exposes readers to the ways our predecessors have thought about and responded to God's *mitzvot* in their day-to-day lives and relationships. Yechiel's is a decidedly religious, heartfelt response to God's presence. He has little interest in propounding a philosophical system that proves God's existence. For him, it is enough to know that God commands us to live and respond in ways that are imbued with values derived from the Torah. His values are not abstractions. They are real, and they can only be seen as real, Yechiel asserts, if they are expressed in our daily lives. We might say that in Yechiel's work, *na'aseh* and *nishmah* coincide. And if we are wise enough to hearken to and act upon Yechiel's teachings, we experience more than just what is called "the good life." What we experience is the presence of God in our lives.

But *Sefer Ma'alot Hamidot* cannot be called a how-to book. Nor does the word *manual* accurately describe it. Yechiel does not tell us exactly how to succeed in business, nor does his work teach us about human relations. He writes of the behaviors that elevate the spirit. His goal is simple: To help his students "be holy as God is holy" by teaching them that the person one sees in the mirror every morning and the person who lives next door are both created *betzelem Elohim*—"in the image of God." Or, as Yechiel might have said to his students, "When you act as a Jew living in covenant with God, this is the way you should strive to be."

About Sefer Ma'alot Hamidot

Let us imagine what one of Yechiel's classes must have been like. Yechiel himself seems to be a kindly man, greeting his students at the door as they enter the classroom one by one. After they have all filed in, Yechiel announces that the *shiur*—"lesson"—will begin shortly. The students notice the room is bright and warm. Filled bookshelves line the walls. As they look more closely, they see hundreds of bound manuscripts with Hebrew, Italian, Latin, Greek, and Aramaic titles.

Each student takes a seat in one of the many chairs surrounding a large wooden carved table, itself a work of art. Nervously, they introduce themselves to one another as they wait for the class to start.

At last, the kindly man who welcomed them takes his seat at the head of the table. He looks each student in the eye, as if he were measuring something hidden deep within them, something that he knows will surface only with the help of a gentle and guiding hand.

Softly, he begins to speak. "*Banai*," he says. "My children, my students. I am Yechiel, the son of Yekutiel, the son of Benyamin Harofe. We have much to learn together. You have studied Torah from the moment you learned how to read. You know much already about your ancestors; you have even begun to study the teachings of our sages' *midrashim* and interpretations of the Talmud.

"But you have also heard the expression *Lo hamidrash ha'ikar ela hama'aseh*—'It is the deeds that count, not the word.' In our discussions, we will try to bring the word and the deed together by asking ourselves some challenging questions: Can we be righteous as Abraham was? Can we pray as Isaac prayed that afternoon in the field? Can we deal with crisis as Joseph did when he found himself alone with Potiphar's wife? Can we find it in our hearts to give others the benefit of the doubt and the opportunity to do *teshuvah*? Can we perform acts of *tzedakah* without losing our humility or jeopardizing the dignity of others?

"Yes, my friends, we have much to do. For we have more to learn than just the texts, more than just the language, more than just the origins of our sacred sources. We must learn to live as God commands, so that the Holy One may dwell among us. We must learn a way of being that is honest and faithful, a way that will make our world a fit resting place for God's presence."

Yechiel pauses. The fidgeting of the students has stopped, their anxieties dissipated by the words of the great scholar. Together, they prepare for the great task ahead of infusing their small corner of creation with *kedushah*.

It may be said that Yechiel was a visionary whose teachings anticipated by several centuries the following saying attributed to the Chasidic Rebbe Zusya: "It is not enough to say Torah; one must *be* it. It is not enough to demonstrate a mastery of the text; one must make Torah a part of one's daily living." Yechiel's purpose is to provide his students with a clearer sense of what being a Jew who lives, works, and relates to others in the presence of God and as a partner in the covenant means.

In essence, Yechiel teaches us how to take our first tentative steps toward holiness, steps whose purpose is to create within us an awareness of the spiritual aspect of every moment.

This introduction to Yechiel's teachings comprises excerpts translated from ten of the twenty-four chapters of *Sefer Ma'alot Hamidot*. The authors recommend that readers study one excerpt at a time and think about it, using the commentary and explanations as a guide. Because Yechiel discusses values that also concerned other sages, this text gives readers a taste of how other teachers within our tradition, teachers with their own perspectives, understood and explained each of the values presented. Finally, in order to appreciate the fact that Yechiel also has much to say to Jews living at the end of the twentieth century about how to bring the presence and influence of the Holy One into our lives, readers will be given the opportunity to apply each of these values to a contemporary situation.

The values that Yechiel teaches are without doubt among the most important we have. He reminds us of this in his foreword to *Sefer Ma'alot Hamidot*: "My essential purpose in this compilation for younger pupils and older students is to teach them about fear of God—*yirat ha-Shamayim*—and the ways of the world—*derech eretz*—so that they may inherit the life of this world and the life of the World to Come and may be seen with favor and intelligence in the eyes of God and other people." Yechiel presents a unified vision of how we should live. According to Yechiel, our consciousness of God's presence must do more than merely influence our actions and interactions. It must be manifest in them.

In short, it is not enough to know. One must do. Yechiel understood that the spiritual development of those seeking to respond to God's presence in this world depended on his challenging them to hear and to do. And there is no doubt that Yechiel intends to challenge us.

In this volume we will study the following ten chapters from *Sefer Ma'alot Hamidot*: *Yediat ha-El*, *Gemilut Chasadim*, *Tzedakah*, *Tefilah*, *Boshet*, *Emunah*, *Temimut*, *Shem Tov*, *Teshuvah*, and *Shalom*. Or, as Yechiel would have said: *Banai bo'u va'alamedchem*—"Come, my students, and I shall teach you." So, with Yechiel at the head of the table, let us begin to learn. And as we study, may God's presence dwell among us.

Yediat ha-El
יְדִיעַת הָאֵל

Since the knowledge of God [*yediat ha-El*] is the "highest" of all virtues and anyone who reaches this level of virtue will subsequently find it easy to attain all of the other levels of spiritual and physical virtue, therefore, I have placed this virtue above all the rest of the virtues found in this book. I have also included with this level of virtue matters that are great principles from the foundations of our religion and the roots of the faith on which the cornerstones of the Torah stand, because they also bring a person to know and recognize his Creator.

My students, come and I will teach you the virtue known as the knowledge of God, who is blessed. Know, my students, that first we must believe and know with clear knowledge—without any doubt or hesitation—that there is God in the world, and God, who is blessed, creates everything. God created the heavens and all of their hosts, the earth and everything on it, the seas and everything in them. And God gives life to all of them with great mercy and kindness. God's creations did not precede God, that God would be beholden to them, but rather they owe God, for God's goodness and kindness is upon them. As it is written: "*Adonai is good to all, and God's mercy is upon all God's creations.*" [Psalms 145:9] And it is written: "*Remember, O God, Your mercy and Your kindness, for they are as old as time.*" [Psalms 25:6] And thus it is written: "*Whoever confronts Me I will compensate,*

בַּעֲבוּר שֶׁמַּעֲלַת הַמִּדָּה הַזֹּאת הִיא מִבְחַר כָּל הַמַּעֲלוֹת, וְכָל מִי שֶׁהִגִּיעַ אֶל מַעֲלַת הַמִּדָּה הַזֹּאת נָקֵל לְהַגִּיעַ אַחֲרֵי כֵן אֶל כָּל שְׁאָר מַעֲלוֹת הַמִּדּוֹת הָרוּחָנִיּוֹת וְהַגּוּפָנִיּוֹת מַעֲלָה אַחַר מַעֲלָה, לְפִיכָךְ הִקְדַּמְתִּי אוֹתָהּ אֶל כָּל שְׁאָר הַמַּעֲלוֹת הַכְּלוּלוֹת בַּסֵּפֶר הַזֶּה. וְכָלַלְתִּי עִם מַעֲלַת הַמִּדָּה הַזֹּאת דְּבָרִים שֶׁהֵם עִקָּרִים גְּדוֹלִים מִיסוֹדוֹת הַדָּת וְשָׁרְשֵׁי הָאֱמוּנָה וַעֲלֵיהֶם פִּנּוֹת הַתּוֹרָה עוֹמְדוֹת, מִפְּנֵי שֶׁגַּם הֵם מְבִיאִים אֶת הָאָדָם לֵידַע וּלְהַכִּיר אֶת בּוֹרְאוֹ.

בָּנַי, בֹּאוּ וַאֲלַמֶּדְכֶם מַעֲלַת יְדִיעַת הָאֵל יִתְבָּרַךְ. דְּעוּ בָנַי, כִּי תְּחִלָּה אָנוּ צְרִיכִין לְהַאֲמִין וְלֵידַע יְדִיעָה בְרוּרָה בְּלִי שׁוּם סָפֵק וְגִמְגּוּם, שֶׁיֵּשׁ אֱלוֹהַּ בָּעוֹלָם, וְהוּא בָּרוּךְ הוּא בּוֹרֵא הַכֹּל. וְהוּא בָּרָא אֶת הַשָּׁמַיִם וְכָל צְבָאָם הָאָרֶץ וְכָל אֲשֶׁר עָלֶיהָ הַיַּמִּים וְכָל אֲשֶׁר בָּהֶם. וְהוּא מְחַיֶּה אֶת כֻּלָּם בְּרֹב רַחֲמָיו וַחֲסָדָיו, וְלֹא מְטוֹבָה קָדְמוּ לוֹ בְּרִיּוֹתָיו, כִּי אִם בְּטוּבוֹ וְחַסְדּוֹ עֲלֵיהֶם, כָּעִנְיָן שֶׁנֶּאֱמַר, טוֹב-יְיָ לַכֹּל וְרַחֲמָיו עַל-כָּל-מַעֲשָׂיו. וְאוֹמֵר, זְכֹר רַחֲמֶיךָ יְיָ וַחֲסָדֶיךָ כִּי מֵעוֹלָם הֵמָּה. וְכֵן הוּא אוֹמֵר, מִי הִקְדִּימַנִי וַאֲשַׁלֵּם תַּחַת כָּל-הַשָּׁמַיִם לִי-הוּא. וְאָמְרוּ חֲכָמֵינוּ בָּאַגָּדָה, זֶה לְשׁוֹנָה, עֲתִידָה בַת-קוֹל לִהְיוֹת מְפוֹצֶצֶת עַל רָאשֵׁי הֶהָרִים

for everything under the heavens is Mine." [Job 41:3] And the sages said in an *aggadah* [legend]: "A heavenly voice [*vat kol*] will cry out in the future on the tops of the mountains and say, 'What did God do? Anyone who has worked with God should come and receive his reward.' And the Holy Spirit says: 'Whoever came before Me, I will compensate. Who praised Me before I gave him breath? Who performed circumcision for Me before I gave him a son? Who made *tzitzit* for Me before I gave him a *talit*? Who made a *mezuzah* for Me before I gave him a house? Who made a parapet for Me before I gave him a roof? Who made a *sukah* for Me before I gave him a yard? Who set apart *leket*, *shichah*, and *peah* before I gave him a field? Who set apart *terumah* and the tithe before I gave him a threshing floor? Who offered a sacrifice before I gave him an animal? I must compensate him. Why? Everything under the heavens is Mine, since everything is Mine and from Mine he gives Me.'" [*Vayikra Rabbah* 27:2]

וְאוֹמֶרֶת מַה פָּעַל אֵל. כָּל מִי שֶׁפָּעַל עִם אֵל יָבוֹא וְיִטוֹל שְׂכָרוֹ. וְרוּחַ־הַקֹּדֶשׁ אוֹמֶרֶת, מִי הִקְדִּימַנִי וַאֲשַׁלֵּם. מִי קִלֵּס לְפָנַי עַד שֶׁלֹּא נָתַתִּי בּוֹ נְשָׁמָה. מִי מָל לְפָנַי עַד שֶׁלֹּא נָתַתִּי לוֹ בֵּן זָכָר. מִי עָשָׂה לְפָנַי צִיצִית עַד שֶׁלֹּא נָתַתִּי לוֹ טַלִּית. מִי עָשָׂה לְפָנַי מְזוּזָה עַד שֶׁלֹּא נָתַתִּי לוֹ בַּיִת. מִי עָשָׂה לְפָנַי מַעֲקֶה עַד שֶׁלֹּא נָתַתִּי לוֹ גַּג. מִי עָשָׂה לְפָנַי סֻכָּה עַד שֶׁלֹּא נָתַתִּי לוֹ חָצֵר. מִי הִנִּיחַ לֶקֶט שִׁכְחָה וּפֵאָה עַד שֶׁלֹּא נָתַתִּי לוֹ שָׂדֶה. מִי הִפְרִישׁ לְפָנַי תְּרוּמָה וּמַעֲשֵׂר עַד שֶׁלֹּא נָתַתִּי לוֹ גֹּרֶן. מִי הִפְרִישׁ לְפָנַי קָרְבָּן עַד שֶׁלֹּא נָתַתִּי לוֹ בְּהֵמָה. עָלַי לְשַׁלֵּם שְׂכָרוֹ. לָמָּה, תַּחַת כָּל הַשָּׁמַיִם לִי הוּא, שֶׁהַכֹּל שֶׁלִּי וּמִשֶּׁלִּי נוֹתֵן לִי.

And further, we must believe and know that the Creator, who is blessed, has no body and no material substance, no shape and no image. As it is written: "You hear the sounds of words, but you see no shape—nothing but a voice." [Deuteronomy 4:12] And the Bible says: "And to whom can you liken God, and to what form can you compare God?" [Isaiah 40:18] And further it says, "'And to whom can you liken Me, that I will be equivalent to it?' says the Holy One." [Isaiah 40:25] And this is true despite the fact that we find many passages in the Bible that contain anthropomorphic terms [*milot gashmiyot*] about the

וְעוֹד צְרִיכִין אָנוּ לְהַאֲמִין וְלֵידַע שֶׁאֵין לַבּוֹרֵא יִתְבָּרַךְ, לֹא גּוּף וְלֹא גֶשֶׁם וְלֹא תְמוּנָה וְלֹא שׁוּם דְּמוּת, כְּעִנְיָן שֶׁנֶּאֱמַר, קוֹל דְּבָרִים אַתֶּם שֹׁמְעִים וּתְמוּנָה אֵינְכֶם רֹאִים זוּלָתִי קוֹל. וְאוֹמֵר, וְאֶל־מִי תְּדַמְּיוּן אֵל וּמַה־דְּמוּת תַּעַרְכוּ־לוֹ? וְכֵן הוּא אוֹמֵר, וְאֶל־מִי תְדַמְּיוּנִי וְאֶשְׁוֶה? יֹאמַר קָדוֹשׁ. וְאַף־עַל־פִּי שֶׁמָּצִינוּ בַּמִּקְרָא מִקְרָאוֹת רַבִּים כְּתוּבִים בָּהֶם מִלּוֹת גַּשְׁמִיּוֹת אֵצֶל הַבּוֹרֵא יִתְבָּרַךְ, כְּעִנְיָן שֶׁנֶּאֱמַר, בְּכָל־מָקוֹם עֵינֵי יְיָ. אַף־יָדִי יָסְדָה אָרֶץ. וְתַחַת רַגְלָיו כְּמַעֲשֵׂה לִבְנַת הַסַּפִּיר. כְּתוּבִים

Creator, who is blessed. For example, it is written: "The eyes of God are everywhere." [Proverbs 15:3] "Even My hand laid the foundation of the earth." [Isaiah 48:13] "Under God's feet there was the likeness of a pavement of sapphire." [Exodus 24:10] "God gave me the two tablets of stone inscribed by the finger of God." [Deuteronomy 9:10] These and many similar passages were only written to explain to human beings in a way that they are able to understand. And similarly, the sages, of blessed memory, said: "The Torah speaks in the language of human beings." [*Berachot* 31b] And all of these are "nicknames" [*kinuyim*—indications about] and comparisons to the Creator. The essential truth is that God has no body or physical image. And the Torah often warns us to keep away from such anthropomorphism. As it is written: "Only beware and watch your souls carefully, since you saw no shape when God spoke to you at Horeb out of the fire." [Deuteronomy 4:15]

בְּאֶצְבַּע אֱלֹהִים. וּמִקְרָאוֹת רַבִּים כַּיּוֹצֵא בָאֵלּוּ, לֹא נִכְתְּבוּ כִּי אִם לְהָבִין לִבְנֵי־אָדָם בְּמַה שֶּׁיּוּכְלוּ לְהָבִין. וְעַל כַּיּוֹצֵא בָזֶה אָמְרוּ חֲכָמֵינוּ זִכְרוֹנָם לִבְרָכָה, דִּבְּרָה תוֹרָה כִּלְשׁוֹן בְּנֵי־אָדָם. וְהַכֹּל כִּנּוּיִים וּמְשָׁלִים אֵצֶל הַבּוֹרֵא. וְעִקַּר הָאֱמֶת, שֶׁהוּא בְּלִי גוּף וּתְמוּנָה גַשְׁמִית. וְהַרְבֵּה הִזְהִירָנוּ בַתּוֹרָה לְהַרְחִיק מִמֶּנּוּ הַגַּשְׁמִיּוּת, כָּעִנְיָן שֶׁנֶּאֱמַר, רַק הִשָּׁמֶר לְךָ וּשְׁמֹר נַפְשְׁךָ מְאֹד כִּי לֹא רְאִיתֶם כָּל־תְּמוּנָה וגו'.

And we must know clearly and unequivocally that the Torah of Moses our teacher, may he rest in peace, is true, and its commandments are true, and the entire text comes from God [*mipi hagevurah*] without addition or deletion, and Moses did not speak it from his own mind. The Torah is true. As it is written: "Your righteousness is righteous for eternity, and your Torah is true." [Psalms 119:142] And the psalmist says: "The teaching of God is perfect, restoring the soul; the testimony of God is honest/faithful, making wise the simple." [Psalms 19:8] And further it says: "Every word of God is pure." [Proverbs 30:5]

וּצְרִיכִין אָנוּ לֵידַע עַל הָאֱמֶת וְהַנָּכוֹן, כִּי תוֹרַת מֹשֶׁה רַבֵּנוּ עָלָיו הַשָּׁלוֹם הִיא אֱמֶת, וּמִצְוֹתֶיהָ אֱמֶת, וְכֻלָּהּ הִיא מִפִּי הַגְּבוּרָה בְּלִי תוֹסֶפֶת וּמִגְרַעַת, וְלֹא אֲמָרָהּ מֹשֶׁה רַבֵּנוּ מִדַּעְתּוֹ. הִיא אֱמֶת, כְּמָה שֶׁנֶּאֱמַר, צִדְקָתְךָ צֶדֶק לְעוֹלָם וְתוֹרָתְךָ אֱמֶת. וְאוֹמֵר, תּוֹרַת יְיָ תְּמִימָה מְשִׁיבַת נָפֶשׁ עֵדוּת יְיָ נֶאֱמָנָה מַחְכִּימַת פֶּתִי. וְכֵן הוּא אוֹמֵר, כָּל־אִמְרַת אֱלוֹהַּ צְרוּפָה וגו'.

3

Commentary

In many synagogues throughout the world, there is an inscription that appears above the ark and faces the Jew every time he or she prays there. It reads, *Da lifnei mi atah omed*—"Know before whom you stand." This charge to "know" God is not just a prerequisite for prayer but a spiritual virtue that should be one of the primary features of living an exemplary Jewish life. The attainment of the knowledge of God is no easy feat. But it is a goal from which no Jew should shy away.

Yechiel opens his book with a discussion of this virtue, which he refers to as the "highest" of all virtues. Why is this so? Because, according to Yechiel, anyone who can reach this spiritual level will be able to reach all the others easily. Yechiel views the knowledge of God, *yediat ha-El*, as an essential principle and the foundation of the organized religion called Judaism. In other words, it is a spiritual virtue that has *religious* implications and consequences. It not only concerns a Jew's inner life; it also affects a Jew's outer life.

The knowledge of God serves as the intellectual cornerstone of faith—the virtue that makes belief in the sanctity and veracity of the Torah possible. But the interrelationship between knowledge and faith is dynamic: Although intellectual apprehension clearly makes believing in God much easier, sometimes faith itself—in its varying degrees—can result in a different kind of knowledge, one that is the product more of spiritual or emotional factors than of purely cognitive ones.

The underlying assumption of *yediat ha-El* is the notion that God exists. Before we can give thought to what constitutes God's essence—i.e., God's nature, attributes, abilities, etc.—we must first establish God's existence. The attainment of knowledge is achieved in stages, ranging from the most basic intellectual building blocks to the most complex concepts and operations. For example, we cannot grasp how respiration works unless we first understand the fundamentals of chemistry. The knowledge of God is no exception: We must know that God is real before any further discussion about God makes any sense.

Following the certainty that God exists in the world comes the understanding that God *created* the world. This notion of God as Creator is one of the central tenets of Jewish faith and one of the most ancient of religious beliefs. Using the images from the first chapter of Genesis, Yechiel argues that God created everything—the heavens and all their hosts, the earth and all its inhabitants, the seas and all their contents. This Creator-God gives life to all that lives and existence to all that exists.

Yet this discussion of God's creative power does little to explain God's *motivation* to create. So Yechiel offers an explanation: God created the world because God is good. Out of God's mercy and kindness—*rachamav vechasadav*, divine attributes that preceded the dawn of creation itself—the world and all of its contents came to be. God had no need to give birth to the world, but because God was merciful and kind, God gave the world the gift of life. The idea of God's benevolence is yet another pillar of Jewish belief.

Up to this point, Yechiel has described three basic features of *yediat ha-El*: the knowledge that God exists, the knowledge that God is a Creator, and the knowledge that God is good.

He now offers a fourth: the knowledge that God is incorporeal. As an immaterial force or being, God has no body, no shape, no image. God has no material substance whatsoever. Although matter exists, it does so only for a short period of time before it begins to rot and decay. God, on the other hand, is eternal and is, therefore, beyond the constraints of matter and the effects of time.

But how does Yechiel reconcile this classical Jewish belief in God's incorporeality with the Bible's descriptions of God, which contain scores of anthropomorphic references and terms? Rather than viewing these images of God as a part of the actual beliefs of the biblical period, as many modern Bible scholars have done, Yechiel claims that they were used not as true presentations or conceptions of God but to help human beings grasp what would otherwise be unfathomable.

Quoting from the Talmud, Yechiel comments that the Torah speaks "in the language of human beings." Whenever we find an image of God in the Bible that is anthropomorphic (e.g., "The eyes of God are everywhere"), we must remind ourselves that such images are just verbal expressions for and indicators of a Truth that is, in reality, beyond expression. Although God has no body or physical image, these are the only images we can use to describe God. It is difficult if not impossible for human beings to conceive of something that transcends our own realm of experience.

The implications are profound. Most important, they point out the limitations of human knowledge. Although we are capable of knowing things, we cannot know all things directly. Our knowledge of God is, therefore, an imperfect and impure kind of knowledge, a knowledge bound by limits and constraints. And if *yediat ha-El* is limited, then in some ways it is closely related to faith—i.e., it is a knowledge that contains an element of belief. We know *that* God is. As to *what* exactly God is or does, we know some things and have our suspicions or hopes about others.

Related to the truth of God's existence is the truth that God is the Creator of the Torah, just as God is the Creator of the world. If, as Yechiel claims, the Torah is the direct "word" of God and is not just the product of Moses and others, then its *mitzvot* are also true, in the sense that they are the revelation of God's will. Such a view establishes the authority of the Torah's commandments and makes obedience of them not just an option but a divine mandate. Thus Yechiel conveys to us how the acquisition of a spiritual virtue like *yediat ha-El* can serve as the gateway not only to the attainment of other virtues but also to the practice of the Jewish religion itself.

YEDIAT HA-EL IN JEWISH PHILOSOPHY

Moses Maimonides, known as the Rambam, was a twelfth-century rabbi, philosopher, theologian, exegete, and physician. He was such a prolific writer that it is hard to refer to any of his books as a magnum opus. The work that comes closest must surely be his great medieval code, the *Mishneh Torah*. This enormous compendium (14 books) of Jewish teachings, rules, and regulations covers every aspect of Jewish living. But before the Rambam addressed the complexities and legalisms of Jewish observance that make up the bulk of his code, he wrote the first of its books, *Sefer ha-Mada*, "Book of Knowledge," which deals exclusively with beliefs and ideas that are related to spirituality in general and to God in particular.

According to the Rambam, "The fundamental principle and pillar of all science is to know that there is a First Being who has brought everything that exists into being."[1] The knowledge of God begins with the understanding that there is a First Being, a Prime Mover, a Cause of all causes. The existence of a First Being (which we call God), a notion that has its roots in Aristotelian philosophy, is the necessary condition for all further discourse about the world. What is the answer to "How did the world come to be?" It came into existence as the result of a Being who created it and set it into motion.

The wonder is that God is able to produce and sustain creatures, objects, and laws (like gravity) that are rooted in time and the physical world without using physical force or power. God created something from nothing. As an eternal and immaterial Being, God paradoxically was able to create both time and matter. This truth is an essential part of *yediat ha-El*. Any references in the Bible to a God who has physical features (e.g., hands, feet, etc.) are merely figures of speech, designed, as Yechiel notes, to make the concept of God's immateriality conceivable to human understanding.

Once a person "contemplates God's great and wondrous acts and creations, obtaining from them a glimpse of God's wisdom, which is beyond compare and infinite,"[2] he or she will be moved to love and fear God. The world itself is a testimony to God's creative power and limitless wisdom. The beauty of the physical world and the mystery of its systems and operations instill in a person a love for their Creator. Yet when that same person contemplates his or her own place in the world and his or her insignificance in the face of such enormity, the opposite emotion—fear and trembling—will occur. Both love and fear are natural responses to *yediat Ha-el*, and both are spiritual virtues of the highest order.

YEDIAT HA-EL IN JEWISH MYSTICISM

The Bible presents us with a God who becomes manifest in different ways: sometimes as fearsome and distant, like the God who appears amidst the smoke, thunder, and lightning at Sinai; sometimes as gentle and personal, like the *kol demamah dakah*—"still small voice"—that spoke to Elijah in the desert. The philosophers, on the other hand, describe a God in terms of intellectual categories, such as omnipotence, omniscience, omnibenevolence—constructs far removed from the realm of human experience.

The Jewish mystics offer an alternate conception of God. In their spiritual system, God is explained not so much as a "being" or an "idea" but rather as a wellspring from which all of God's powers emanate. These emanations, known as the 10 *sefirot* or "spheres," flow out of the Godhead, which is referred to as *Ein Sof*—"That which has no limit." The Godhead in itself is unknown and unknowable. Since it is a reality beyond human thought, all we can know of it are the emanations that spring from it, which, taken together, constitute the God of religion, the God that we human beings can understand and worship.

In the sixteenth century, a later Kabbalist, Rabbi Isaac Luria, confronted the question "How could something Infinite (*Ein Sof*) have produced that which is finite (the world)?" In an effort to address this problem, Luria developed the creation myth of *tzimtzum*—"contraction"—the idea that God's first act had to be one of contraction and withdrawal before the world could come into being. If God's infinity fills all of reality, then the only way to make room for other realities (e.g., people, animals, and worlds) is for God to take a step, so to speak, back.

In the eighteenth century, Rabbi Dov Baer, the Maggid of Mezhirech, took this notion of *tzimtzum* and transformed it. Rather than merely offering us an explanation for the story of creation, he argued that divine contraction also gives us a model for grasping the phenomenon of *yediat ha-El*. In characteristic fashion, the Maggid created the following parable to convey his point:

> It is written, "Make two cherubim (*keruvim*)" [Exodus 25:18]; but as our sages said, *keravya* [a play on the word *ke-ravya*—"like an infant"]. Such is the way of the father who, because of his love for the child, distorts his speech and speaks in the manner of a child or contracts his intellect into that of the child. We, therefore, find that the father is on the level of [the intellect of] the son, and that explains "make two cherubim."[3]

Whereas Luria's discussion of *tzimtzum* explains how the world came to be, the Maggid uses the concept to describe how a finite mind can come to know a mind that is infinite. Just as a parent must "shrink" his or her intellect and garble his or her speech (with words like "goo-goo" and "ga-ga") in order to communicate with an infant, so God must "contract" God's infinite mind if intellectual contact between God and human beings is to occur. Divine knowledge in this case is not transmitted directly, since it would be incomprehensible to us, but through the "filter" of God's restraint.

The motivation for this act of self-contraction, as the Maggid's interpretation makes plain, is love—the love of God for humanity, which the Maggid compares to the love of a parent for his or her child. Although it might seem paradoxical that God can only reveal divine knowledge through an initial act of concealment (*tzimtzum*), that is the only way that understanding between two partners of such unequal powers can take place. Thus, for the Maggid, *yediat ha-El* is more of a *spiritual* phenomenon than an intellectual one. Without an act of revelation by God, no knowledge of God would be possible.

Yediat ha-El: A Case Study

It is clear that the virtue of *yediat ha-El* serves as a starting point for both the discussion and the practice of Judaism. By putting the chapter about this virtue first in a book of virtues, Yechiel makes clear its position in the chain of spiritual priorities. For a great many people today, however, the acquisition of this primary virtue is problematic, making the attainment of all the other virtues—and thus the development of our spiritual selves—difficult. No one who is serious about living a Jewish life can ignore this key foundation of the Jewish consciousness.

THE WRITER

Ludwig is a successful free-lance writer. He writes articles and essays for various magazines and journals and in his spare time works on a novel that has been gnawing at him for years. Ludwig is exceedingly well-read, and his circle of friends is equally literate and intellectual. When their group gets together, they discuss everything from the theater to politics to the economy. One evening, the discussion turns to the topic of God and religion.

While some of his friends entertain the notion that there might in fact be a God, Ludwig will hear none of it. Not only is there no "proof" that God exists, he claims, but all of human experience—especially the existence of suffering—contradicts the traditional idea of a God who is an all-powerful and all-good Being. Moreover, Ludwig refuses to believe in the God of the Bible, a God who rewards and punishes, a God who grows angry and jealous, a God who speaks and sees. For him, this kind of God is no less primitive than the gods of the Greek pantheon or the idols of the ancient Near East, nor is the religion that originated with this God any more worthy of still being observed.

—— WHAT MIGHT CHANGE LUDWIG'S MIND? ——

QUESTIONS FOR DISCUSSION

1. What kind of "proof" do you think Ludwig would require to make him believe in the reality of God?
2. Is Ludwig correct in his claim that the existence of suffering and the classic idea of an omnipotent, omnibenevolent God are mutually exclusive? How might this apparent problem be resolved?
3. Ludwig equates the biblical conceptions of God (which refer to God's inclinations, emotions, physical abilities, etc.) with those of idolatrous religious traditions. How might you respond to his comparison? How might those biblical descriptions be interpreted in nonliteral ways?
4. What kind of connection is Ludwig making between the reality of God and the validity of religion? Do you agree with it?
5. Is it possible to ground the authenticity and observance of religion on anything other than the existence of God? If so, on what?
6. Do you think that there are alternative conceptions of God to the ones Ludwig mentions? Do you believe in God? If so, what is your own conception of God?

---

[1] *Mishneh Torah, Book 1, Yesodei ha-Torah*, 1:1
[2] Ibid., 1:2
[3] *Shemuah Tovah* (Warsaw, 1938), p.73b

Gemilut Chasadim
גְּמִילוּת־חֲסָדִים

Come, my students, and I will instruct you in the virtue of loving-kindness. You must know, my students, that the virtue of loving-kindness [*gemilut chasadim*] is beloved before God, and because of it, one is able to earn life in this world and in the World to Come. And not only that, but the world is settled for anyone who does kindness to others. As it is written: "May he dwell in God's presence forever; appoint mercy and truth [*chesed* and *emet*] to guard him." [Psalms 61:8] And the sages, of blessed memory, said: "The world is sustained by three things—by Torah, by service, and by acts of loving-kindness." [*Pirkei Avot* 1:2]

Great is the virtue of *gemilut chasadim* because it is one of the thirteen attributes ascribed to God. As it is written: "*Adonai, Adonai*...long-suffering and abundant in kindness [*rav chesed*]." [Exodus 34:6]

Our sages, of blessed memory, said: "And abundant kindness [*rav chesed*] means a staff tilted toward kindness." [*Rosh Hashanah* 17a] That is to say that if a person seems half innocent and half guilty, God weighs down the scale on the side of innocence. And this is a great kindness that the Holy One, who is blessed, does with God's creations, that God judges them innocent in order to bring them to the World to Come. And about this David said: "I was low, and God saved me." [Psalms 116:6] And we find that the Holy One was busy with acts of loving-kindness, for this is what the sages, of blessed memory, said: "The

בָּנַי, בֹּאוּ וַאֲלַמֶּדְכֶם מַעֲלַת גְּמִילוּת־חֲסָדִים. דְּעוּ בָנַי, כִּי מַעֲלַת גְּמִילוּת־חֲסָדִים מַעֲלָה חֲבִיבָה לִפְנֵי הַמָּקוֹם, וּבַעֲבוּרָהּ יִזְכֶּה הָאָדָם לִקְנוֹת חַיֵּי הָעוֹלָם הַזֶּה וְחַיֵּי הָעוֹלָם הַבָּא. וְלֹא עוֹד אֶלָּא שֶׁכָּל מִי שֶׁהוּא עוֹשֶׂה חֶסֶד עִם הַבְּרִיּוֹת, הֲרֵי הָעוֹלָם מִתְיַשֵּׁב בִּשְׁבִילוֹ, כָּעִנְיָן שֶׁנֶּאֱמַר, יֵשֵׁב עוֹלָם לִפְנֵי אֱלֹהִים חֶסֶד וֶאֱמֶת מַן יִנְצְרֻהוּ. וְאָמְרוּ חֲכָמֵינוּ זִכְרוֹנָם לִבְרָכָה, עַל שְׁלֹשָׁה דְבָרִים הָעוֹלָם עוֹמֵד, עַל הַתּוֹרָה, וְעַל הָעֲבוֹדָה, וְעַל גְּמִילוּת־חֲסָדִים.

גְּדוֹלָה מַעֲלַת גְּמִילוּת־חֲסָדִים, שֶׁהִיא אַחַת מִשְּׁלֹשׁ־עֶשְׂרֵה מִדּוֹת שֶׁנִּתְיַחֵס בָּהֶן הַבּוֹרֵא, כָּעִנְיָן שֶׁנֶּאֱמַר, יְיָ, יְיָ וְגוֹ' אֶרֶךְ אַפַּיִם וְרַב־חֶסֶד וְגוֹ'.

וְאָמְרוּ חֲכָמֵינוּ זִכְרוֹנָם לִבְרָכָה, וְרַב־חֶסֶד, מַטֶּה כְּלַפֵּי חֶסֶד. כְּלוֹמַר, שֶׁאִם הָאָדָם מֶחֱצָה זַכַּאי וּמֶחֱצָה חַיָּב, מַכְרִיעַ כַּף שֶׁל זְכִיּוֹת עַל כַּף שֶׁל חוֹבוֹת וּמְזַכֶּה אוֹתוֹ בַּדִּין. וְזֶהוּ חֶסֶד גָּדוֹל שֶׁהַקָּדוֹשׁ־בָּרוּךְ־הוּא עוֹשֶׂה עִם בְּרִיּוֹתָיו שֶׁמְּזַכֶּה אוֹתָן כְּדֵי לַהֲבִיאָן לְחַיֵּי הָעוֹלָם הַבָּא. וְעַל זֶה אָמַר דָּוִד, דַּלּוֹתִי וְלִי יְהוֹשִׁיעַ. וּמָצִינוּ שֶׁהַקָּדוֹשׁ־בָּרוּךְ־הוּא בְּעַצְמוֹ נִתְעַסֵּק בִּגְמִילוּת־חֲסָדִים, שֶׁכָּךְ אָמְרוּ חֲכָמֵינוּ זִכְרוֹנָם לִבְרָכָה, תּוֹרָה תְּחִלָּתָהּ גְּמִילוּת־חֲסָדִים וְסוֹפָהּ גְּמִילוּת־חֲסָדִים. תְּחִלָּתָהּ

9

Torah begins and ends with *gemilut chasadim*." The Torah begins with *gemilut chasadim*. As it is written: "God made tunics of leather for the first man and his wife and clothed them." [Genesis 3:21] And the Torah ends with an act of loving-kindness. As it is written: "And God buried him [Moses] at Gai." [Deuteronomy 34:6] And not only that, but the entire world is founded upon mercy [*chesed*]. As it is written: "I declare the world will be established on *chesed*" [Psalms 89:3] and "Remember Your mercy and Your kindness, for they are as old as time." [Psalms 25:6]

Acts of loving-kindness are greater than sacrifices. As it is written: "For I desire kindness/faithfulness/piety and not burnt offerings." [Hosea 6:6]

גְּמִילוּת־חֲסָדִים, דִּכְתִיב, וַיַּעַשׂ יְיָ אֱלֹהִים לְאָדָם וּלְאִשְׁתּוֹ כָּתְנוֹת עוֹר וַיַּלְבִּשֵׁם. וְסוֹפָהּ גְּמִילוּת־חֲסָדִים, דִּכְתִיב, וַיִּקְבֹּר אֹתוֹ בַגַּיְא. וְלֹא עוֹד אֶלָּא שֶׁכָּל הָעוֹלָם כֻּלּוֹ נִבְנָה בְחֶסֶד, כָּעִנְיָן שֶׁנֶּאֱמַר, כִּי־אָמַרְתִּי עוֹלָם חֶסֶד יִבָּנֶה. וְכֵן הוּא אוֹמֵר, זְכֹר רַחֲמֶיךָ יְיָ וַחֲסָדֶיךָ כִּי מֵעוֹלָם הֵמָּה.

גְּדוֹלָה גְּמִילוּת־חֲסָדִים יוֹתֵר מִן הַקָּרְבָּנוֹת, שֶׁנֶּאֱמַר, כִּי חֶסֶד חָפַצְתִּי וְלֹא־זָבַח.

And what is *gemilut chasadim*? That a person will be merciful, having compassion for others, just as God is merciful and full of compassion. As it is written: "*Adonai*, *Adonai*, a God compassionate and gracious." [Exodus 34:6] And as it is written: "And God's mercy is on all God's creations." [Psalms 145:9] And this virtue is also ascribed to Israelites. For this is as the sages, of blessed memory, taught: "Whoever has compassion for others is surely a descendant of Abraham, our father." [*Betzah* 32b] And a person should be kind to everyone—to the rich and to the poor, to the living and to the dead. And a person should draw the estranged near and the near even closer. If they need support, he should support them; if they need clothing, he should clothe them; if they need a place to stay, he should take them into his home; if they are in need of money, he should lend it to them; if they need to borrow an item, he should lend it to

וּמַהוּ גְּמִילוּת־חֲסָדִים? שֶׁיִּהְיֶה הָאָדָם רַחֲמָן מְרַחֵם עַל הַבְּרִיּוֹת כְּדֶרֶךְ שֶׁהַבּוֹרֵא יִתְבָּרַךְ הוּא רַחֲמָן וּמָלֵא רַחֲמִים, כָּעִנְיָן שֶׁנֶּאֱמַר, יְיָ, יְיָ אֵל רַחוּם וְחַנּוּן. וְכֵן הוּא אוֹמֵר, וְרַחֲמָיו עַל־כָּל־מַעֲשָׂיו. וּבְמַעֲלַת הַמִּדָּה הַזֹּאת נִתְיַחֲסוּ בָהּ בְּנֵי־יִשְׂרָאֵל. שֶׁכָּךְ אָמְרוּ חֲכָמֵינוּ זִכְרוֹנָם לִבְרָכָה, כָּל הַמְרַחֵם עַל הַבְּרִיּוֹת, בְּיָדוּעַ שֶׁהוּא מִזַּרְעוֹ שֶׁל אַבְרָהָם אָבִינוּ. וְשֶׁיְּהֵא גּוֹמֵל חֶסֶד עִם כָּל אָדָם, לַעֲשִׁירִים וְלָעֲנִיִּים, לַחַיִּים וְלַמֵּתִים. וְשֶׁיְּהֵא מְקָרֵב אֶת הָרְחוֹקִים, וְכָל־שֶׁכֵּן הַקְּרוֹבִים. הָיוּ צְרִיכִין לְפַרְנָסָה, מְפַרְנְסָן. לִכְסוּת, מַלְבִּישָׁן. לְאַכְסַנְיָא, מַכְנִיסָן בְּתוֹךְ בֵּיתוֹ. לִלְווֹת, מַלְוֶה לָהֶן. לִשְׁאוֹל, מַשְׁאִילָן. לְלִמּוּד תּוֹרָה, מְלַמְּדָן. לְהוֹכִיחַ, מוֹכִיחָן. מְדַבֵּר בְּטוֹבָתָן, וּמַעֲלִים עֵינָיו מִמּוּמֵיהֶן. בִּזְמַן שֶׁהֵן שְׂמֵחִין, שָׂמֵחַ עִמָּהֶן. וּבִזְמַן שֶׁהֵן עֲצֵבִין, מְשַׁדְּלָן

10

them; if they need to study Torah, he should teach it to them; if they need to be rebuked, he should rebuke them. He should speak well of them and ignore their blemishes. When they are happy, he should be happy with them. And when they are sad, he should cheer them up. When he sees a person wasting his possessions and denigrating himself, he should draw that person near to him and admonish him. Thus it is with everything that one sees in one's friend. A person should judge himself as if he were in his friend's shoes. As it is written: "Love your neighbor as thyself." [Leviticus 19:18] And he should do kindness to every person, one who merits kindness and one who does not appear to merit kindness. As one sage said: "Do kindness to one who deserves it and to one who does not deserve it as well, because if he deserves the kindness, you will have placed kindness where it belongs, and if he does not deserve the kindness, you deserve it, because the Creator commanded you to do goodness and kindness." And another sage said: "The best type of kindness is one done before it is requested." Thus a person should accustom himself to repay kindness to one who has done him a kindness in order that he will not be considered ungrateful. Since it is comfortable/fitting for a person when others do kindness for him when he needs them, so it is fitting for a person to do kindness for others when they need it.

Therefore, my students, be careful and diligent with this important virtue in order that you will merit the presence of *Shechinah* [the Divine] and bask in its glow. As it is written: "Then I will behold Your face in righteousness. I will be filled with the vision of You when I awake." [Psalms 17:15] May God with great mercy enable us to succeed in this virtue.

בִּדְבָרִים. רָאָה אוֹתוֹ מַפְקִיר נְכָסָיו וּמְגַנֶּה אֶת עַצְמוֹ, מְקָרְבוֹ אֶצְלוֹ וּמַזְהִירוֹ. וְכֵן בְּכָל דָּבָר וְדָבָר שֶׁהוּא רוֹאֶה בַּחֲבֵרוֹ, יְהִי דָן בְּעַצְמוֹ כְּאִלּוּ הִגִּיעַ לִמְקוֹמוֹ שֶׁל חֲבֵרוֹ, כָּעִנְיָן שֶׁנֶּאֱמַר, וְאָהַבְתָּ לְרֵעֲךָ כָּמוֹךָ. וְיַעֲשֶׂה חֶסֶד עִם כָּל אָדָם, עִם מִי שֶׁרָאוּי לַעֲשׂוֹת עִמּוֹ חֶסֶד וְעִם מִי שֶׁאֵינוֹ רָאוּי לַעֲשׂוֹת עִמּוֹ חָסֶד. כְּמוֹ שֶׁאָמַר חָכָם אֶחָד, עֲשֵׂה חֶסֶד עִם מִי שֶׁרָאוּי לוֹ וְעִם מִי שֶׁאֵינוֹ רָאוּי לוֹ. כִּי אִם יִהְיֶה רָאוּי, תְּשִׂימֶנּוּ בִּמְקוֹמוֹ. וְאִם הוּא לֹא יִהְיֶה רָאוּי לוֹ, אַתָּה רָאוּי לוֹ, כִּי הַבּוֹרֵא צִוְּךָ לַעֲשׂוֹת הַטּוֹב וְהֶחָסֶד. וְאָמַר אַחֵר, מֵיטַב חֲסָדֶיךָ מַה שֶׁתַּקְדִּים בְּלֹא שְׁאֵילָה. וְכֵן יַרְגִּיל אָדָם עַצְמוֹ לְשַׁלֵּם טוֹבָה לְמִי שֶׁגָּמַל עִמּוֹ טוֹבָה, כְּדֵי שֶׁלֹּא יִהְיֶה מִכְּפוּיֵי הַטּוֹבָה. שֶׁכְּשֵׁם שֶׁנּוֹחַ לוֹ לְאָדָם שֶׁיִּהוּ כָּל הַבְּרִיּוֹת גּוֹמְלִין עִמּוֹ חֶסֶד בְּשָׁעָה שֶׁהוּא צָרִיךְ לָהֶם, כָּךְ הוּא רָאוּי לִגְמוֹל חֶסֶד לְכָל אָדָם בְּשָׁעָה שֶׁהֵן צְרִיכִין לוֹ.

לָכֵן בָּנַי, הֱווּ זְהִירִין וּזְרִיזִין בְּמַעֲלַת הַמִּדָּה הַחֲשׁוּבָה הַזֹּאת, כְּדֵי שֶׁתִּזְכּוּ לְהַקְבִּיל פְּנֵי שְׁכִינָה וְלֵהָנוֹת מִזִּיוָהּ, כָּעִנְיָן שֶׁנֶּאֱמַר, אֲנִי בְּצֶדֶק אֶחֱזֶה פָנֶיךָ אֶשְׂבְּעָה בְהָקִיץ תְּמוּנָתֶךָ. הָאֵל יַצְלִיחֵנוּ בָהּ בְּרַחֲמָיו הָרַבִּים.

Commentary

One of the very first lessons in *Pirkei Avot*, the classic testimony of the rabbinic worldview, is that the world stands on three things—the Torah, divine service, and acts of loving-kindness (*gemilut chasadim*). By stating that *gemilut chasadim* is one of the three pillars that support and sustain the world, the rabbis are saying that in addition to its being a spiritual virtue, *gemilut chasadim* also has existential value. It is one of the foundations of existence.

The concept of *gemilut chasadim* is usually translated as "acts of loving-kindness" or "loving acts of kindness." The root of the word *chasadim* is *chesed*, which means "grace" or "mercy." Thus the virtue of *gemilut chasadim* intimates the act of relating to other people by going beyond what is normative or even what is fair. It involves doing *more* than what is called for.

Yechiel connects the notion of *gemilut chasadim* to the promise of future reward, maintaining that since the person who performs loving acts of kindness is beloved by God, that person will merit a portion of this world, as well as the World to Come. God created the world not because God had to but through an act of love. And when we perform acts of loving-kindness toward others, we become like God, active participants in the constant *re*-creation of our world.

Gemilut chasadim is one of the thirteen attributes of God. These attributes are delineated in Exodus 34:6-7.

1. and 2. *Adonai, Adonai,* traditionally interpreted as God's attribute of mercy. This attribute is repeated to show that God is merciful both before and after people sin and repent.
3. *El,* meaning God's sovereignty over all things.
4. "Compassionate" (*rachum*), referring to God's sympathy to suffering.
5. "Gracious" (*chanun*), interpreted as God's helpful and loving concern.
6. "Slow to anger" (*erech apayim*), referring to God's propensity to give people the chance to repent.
7. "Abounding in kindness" (*rav chesed*), implying that God is more kind than people often deserve.
8. "Full of truth" (*emet*), since God is real and the ultimate Source of truth.
9. "Extending kindness to the thousandth generation" (*notzer chesed la'alafim*), because God remembers and rewards human merit.
10, 11, and 12. "Forgiving iniquity, transgression, and sin" (*nosei avon vafesha vechata'ah*), because God is capable of forgiving all manner of wrongdoing.
13. "Yet God does not remit all punishment" (*venakeh lo yenakeh*), reminding us that there are limits to God's mercy.

The divine attributes begin with a statement about God's mercy but close with a statement about the limitations of that mercy. The attribute of *rav chesed*, which Yechiel equates with *gemilut chasadim*, appears in the midpoint of this list and, as a result, serves as the linchpin between mercy and justice. Just as loving-kindness supports and sustains the world, so, too, does it balance the different aspects of the divine personality.

Yechiel gives examples of what the attribute "abounding in kindness" means. First, it includes giving others the benefit of the doubt when their characters are being called into question. If our judgment of a person wavers between innocence and guilt, we must favor his or her innocence, just as God favors our innocence when we stand in judgment before God. Since Judaism views human nature as essentially good, as opposed to sinful, we must assume that a person whose moral character is unclear to us is predominantly good.

Second, just as God clothed Adam and Eve at the beginning of the Book of Genesis, so, too, we have a responsibility to clothe the naked—that is, the poor and impoverished. Third, just as God buried Moses at the end of the Book of Deuteronomy, so must we fulfill the *mitzvah* of burying the dead. The world does more than just stand on acts of *gemilut chasadim*; such acts function as sacred quotation marks, framing the beginning and the ending of the Torah and revealing to us the will of God.

Yechiel notes that acts of *gemilut chasadim* are "greater" than sacrifices because what God truly desires from us is ethical service more than ritual service. And it is acts of loving-kindness that connect today's people of Israel with Abraham, the paradigm of this virtue and the father of our people. Thus loving-kindness represents the defining characteristic of the Jewish people: Through the imitation of Abraham, Jews connect themselves to their ancient past.

The Jew who acts like Abraham will show kindness toward others in an unconditional manner, irrespective of whether or not they deserve such treatment. It is not another's "merit" that should motivate a person to perform acts of *gemilut chasadim*. Rather, we should perform such acts simply because that is the right thing to do—i.e., because God commands us to do them. A Jew does not sit in judgment of others. If God can offer us—we who are weak, who err, who sin—unconditional love, then how can we show anything less to others?

GEMILUT CHASADIM IN JEWISH PIETISM

Judah the Pious was perhaps the most significant personality in a small circle of medieval Jewish pietists known as the Chasidei Ashkenaz. What distinguishes this group, both in terms of its writings and its behavior, is its zealous devotion to the spiritual life. One of this circle's best-known books, *Otzar Sefer Chasidim*, was written by Judah in the thirteenth century. A guidebook to the principles of Jewish piety, it encompasses an immense range of religious concepts.

The concept of loving-kindness is pivotal to the teachings of Judah, who, like Yechiel, cites Abraham as one of the virtue's exemplars. It is no coincidence that these two great teachers refer to Abraham in this way. In many works of Jewish ethics—and especially in the literature of the Chasidei Ashkenaz—Abraham serves as the very paradigm of moral excellence and spiritual piety.

Judah writes:

> Abraham converted many strangers but was reluctant to marry among them because they were once idolaters; in spite of this, if they were modest and performed acts of loving-kindness, he would allow them to marry into his family.[1]

Judah bases this view of Abraham as proselytizer on an interpretation of a biblical verse (Genesis 12:5) by Rashi, the great medieval commentator. Judah seems to suggest that allegiance to the Jewish faith or even to the Jewish way of life is not sufficient for full "citizenship" in *K'lal Yisrael*—the "Community of Israel." The prerequisite for that and for the right to perpetuate the Jewish people is manifestation of the behavior that distinguishes Jews from other nations—modesty and *gemilut chasadim*.

Judah also claims that *gemilut chasadim* is a prerequisite for personal salvation. He writes:

> When [God] decrees a harsh judgment [on a person] and the punishments have already arrived, if that person lacks great merit, he or she will not be saved. Therefore, one needs Torah, *gemilut chasadim*, and prayer—and great merit—in order to be saved.[2]

This passage echoes the *Unetaneh Tokef* prayer in the Rosh Hashanah liturgy. Its message is clear: Although it is God who ultimately determines our fate ("who shall live and who shall die.../who shall be poor and who shall be rich..."), our own behavior can still save us ("but repentance, prayer, and *tzedakah* can annul the severity of the decree"). Judah makes a similar claim. Although he replaces repentance and charity with Torah and *gemilut chasadim*, the point that meritorious action holds radical power is the same. It is our best weapon in our struggle to alter our destinies and it is the key to the salvation of our souls.

GEMILUT CHASADIM IN JEWISH THOUGHT

Judah Loew of Prague, the Maharal, was a pivotal figure in the history of Jewish thought. It was this sixteenth-century rabbi who served as a conduit between classical forms of Kabbalah and their later, more "humanistic" manifestations in early chasidic teaching. One of his works, *Netivot Olam*, "Paths of the World," is a veritable encyclopedia of Jewish religious concepts.

The Maharal explores in detail the virtue of *gemilut chasadim*. He opens his analysis of this concept in the following way:

> Whoever performs acts of loving-kindness for other human beings will in turn have God, may God be blessed, bestow upon him mercy [in order to] pardon his sins.... When a human being performs acts of loving-kindness and shows goodness toward other creatures, God will do likewise and show that person the attribute of mercy [which will] absolve him of and forgive him for his sins.[3]

The Maharal claims that there is a causal connection between the kindness that people show one another and the kindness that God shows us. (This is consistent with one of the basic tenets of Jewish mystical thought, namely, that the actions we take in the "lower world" have a direct influence on divine behavior in the "upper world.") The kindness that God bestows upon us takes a specific form—*chesed* or "mercy/grace." It is this quality that "clears our account" and absolves us of our sins.

Forgiveness for our sins is one of the greatest gifts that God can give us. Yet we have the ability to "influence" God's decision about whether or not divine pardon will be granted to us. We are told *that* such a dynamic is possible, but we are not told precisely *how* it operates. The Maharal addresses this issue in the following passage:

> A person of *gemilut chasadim* contains within him absolute goodness, for he shows goodness to others. Someone like this may possess the title and delicacy of a material substance, but he is not completely material, since matter cannot influence but only receive…. One who performs acts of loving-kindness lacks the quality of corporeality but embodies instead the cleansing of matter. Through [*gemilut chasadim*] he cleanses and purifies the body from sin. Therefore, with mercy God will pardon his transgressions.[4]

The gift of God's mercy is dependent upon human action. We must transcend our material nature—the fact that we are flesh and blood—before God will pardon our sins. *Gemilut chasadim* helps us to achieve this end. How can loving-kindness elevate a person to such a lofty height? It does so through a kind of personal metamorphosis, by transforming our essential nature from a material one into a spiritual one.

A person who is a *gomel chasadim* is thoroughly good. By demonstrating only goodness toward others, the *gomel chasadim* becomes infused with it. Thus while he or she remains a human "being" and retains corporeality, in essence that person reaches beyond his or her physical nature. As the Maharal notes, sheer matter itself cannot influence or affect other objects but can only receive some value (e.g., nutrition or momentum) from them. On the other hand, since deeds of loving-kindness *do* influence and affect other people, the person who performs them and in turn becomes defined by them is able to "transcend" the mere matter that encases his or her soul.

Although the *gomel chasadim* is unable to escape the frailty of the human body, he or she can break through the physical state and enter a more spiritual one. Acts of loving-kindness "cleanse" the body of its physicality and "purify" it of its sinful desires. This process of spiritual purification prepares the soul for divine mercy and makes it worthy of God's forgiveness.

Gemilut Chasadim: A Case Study

It is clear that Yechiel regards loving-kindness, whether it is manifested through action or in attitude, as an essential component of the Jewish character. The Jew who expresses or embodies *gemilut chasadim* exemplifies what is best in the Jewish value system, especially as it relates to other people. But how can contemporary Jews exhibit this attribute through personal practice?

TO CATCH A THIEF

Rebecca works for a medical supplies company that distributes equipment to local and national hospitals. She spends most of her time working in an office cubicle in front of a computer. In the cubicle next to her sits Kerry, whom she does not like nor particularly trust, mainly because he has a big mouth. One day, after returning to her cubicle from the washroom, Rebecca discovers that her purse, which she always hangs over her chair, is missing.

The office in which Rebecca works is a large, open area and is usually quite busy, with strangers coming and going throughout the day. Rebecca realizes that she was foolish for having left her purse unattended, and she also knows that almost anyone could have taken it. But because Kerry sits right next to her and because she does not trust him, she immediately suspects him.

———— HOW SHOULD REBECCA PROCEED? ————

QUESTIONS FOR DISCUSSION

1. If Kerry is the first person Rebecca informs about the theft of her purse, what should she say to him? What might the consequences of an accusatory tone or statement be?

2. Does Rebecca have grounds to suspect that Kerry might be the thief?

3. Do you think that Rebecca's dislike of Kerry has any bearing on her suspicions? What about the fact that she distrusts him?

4. Although it is true that Rebecca has no proof that Kerry took her purse, he certainly had access and ample opportunity to commit the crime. If Rebecca starts asking him questions about the theft, is she making any presumptions about his moral culpability?

5. How might Rebecca's presumption of Kerry's guilt affect her way of relating to other people?

6. According to Yechiel, even if Kerry were guilty, what must Rebecca first presume about his character?

7. Do you agree with Yechiel's propensity to favor innocence over guilt and good over evil? Is this a realistic way to view human nature?

---

1 *Otzar Sefer Chasidim* (Jerusalem, 1992), *Gemilut Chasadim*
2 Ibid.
3 *Netivot Olam* (B'nei B'rak, 1980), vol. 1, 3:1
4 Ibid.

Tzedakah
צְדָקָה

Come, my students, and I will teach you about the virtue of righteousness. Know, my students, that the virtue of righteousness [*tzedakah*] is a great virtue and reaches God's throne. Thus our sages, of blessed memory, said, "They asked Solomon, How great is the strength/power of *tzedakah*? He said to them, Go out and see how David my father explained it—'He gave freely to the poor; his beneficence [*tzidkato*] lasts forever, his horn will be exalted in honor [*bechavod*].' [Psalms 112:9] That it ascends and elevates itself toward God's throne [*kisei hakavod*]." [*Baba Batra* 10b]

בָּנַי, בֹּאוּ וַאֲלַמֶּדְכֶם מַעֲלַת הַצְּדָקָה. דְּעוּ בָנַי, כִּי מַעֲלַת הַצְּדָקָה הִיא מַעֲלָה גְּדוֹלָה וּמַגַּעַת עַד כִּסֵּא הַכָּבוֹד. שֶׁכָּךְ אָמְרוּ חֲכָמֵינוּ זִכְרוֹנָם לִבְרָכָה, שָׁאֲלוּ אֶת שְׁלֹמֹה, עַד הֵיכָן כֹּחָהּ שֶׁל צְדָקָה? אָמַר לָהֶן, צְאוּ וּרְאוּ מַה פֵּרַשׁ דָּוִד אַבָּא, פִּזַּר נָתַן לָאֶבְיוֹנִים צִדְקָתוֹ עֹמֶדֶת לָעַד קַרְנוֹ תָרוּם בְּכָבוֹד. שֶׁעוֹלָה וּמִתְרוֹמֶמֶת עַד כִּסֵּא הַכָּבוֹד.

Tzedakah is beloved before God. For anyone who does *tzedakah* with his friend, it is considered as if he had breathed life into his friend's spirit. And not only that, but anyone who regularly does *tzedakah* merits and earns for himself a share in this world and in the World to Come. As it is written: "The road of *tzedakah* leads to life, and by way of its path there is no death." [Proverbs 12:28] When one sees a needy person who has nothing to eat and one gives him a coin, and the poor man buys a piece of bread with it and eats and his spirit returns to him, it is as if this [act] revived him. Because had it not been for this [act of *tzedakah*], the needy one might have died of hunger. Thus "the road of

חֲבִיבָה הִיא הַצְּדָקָה לִפְנֵי הַמָּקוֹם. שֶׁכָּל הָעוֹשֶׂה צְדָקָה עִם חֲבֵרוֹ, מַעֲלִין עָלָיו כְּאִלּוּ הֶחֱיָה אֶת נַפְשׁוֹ. וְלֹא עוֹד אֶלָּא, שֶׁכָּל הָרָגִיל בִּצְדָקָה, זוֹכֶה וְקוֹנֶה לוֹ חַיֵּי הָעוֹלָם-הַזֶּה וְחַיֵּי הָעוֹלָם-הַבָּא, כָּעִנְיָן שֶׁנֶּאֱמַר, בְּאֹרַח צְדָקָה חַיִּים וְדֶרֶךְ נְתִיבָה אַל-מָוֶת. שֶׁבִּזְמַן שֶׁאָדָם רוֹאֶה אֶת הֶעָנִי שֶׁאֵין לוֹ מַה יֹּאכַל וְנוֹתֵן לוֹ פְּרוּטָה וְלָקַח מִמֶּנָּה פַּת וְאוֹכֵל וְנַפְשׁוֹ שָׁבָה עָלָיו, נִמְצָא שֶׁזֶּה הֶחֱיָה אוֹתוֹ. שֶׁאִלְמָלֵא זֶה, שֶׁמָּא הָיָה מֵת בָּרָעָב. הֱוֵי, בְּאֹרַח צְדָקָה חַיִּים. שֶׁכָּל הָעוֹשֶׂה צְדָקָה עִם חֲבֵרוֹ, מַעֲלִין עָלָיו כְּאִלּוּ הֶחֱיָה אוֹתוֹ. וְדֶרֶךְ נְתִיבָה אַל-

tzedakah leads to life." So anyone who does *tzedakah* with another elevates him as if he had given him life. "And by way of its path there is no death" means that anyone who regularly does *tzedakah* throws off from himself the angel of death so that it cannot overcome him, even if he had been sentenced to death. And so the verse says: "The treasures of the wicked will not help them, but charity saves from death." [Proverbs 10:2] And not only that, but it remains for him for the World to Come, that he will not die. As it is written: "And by way of its path there is no death." [Proverbs 12:28]

מָוֶת, שֶׁכָּל הָרָגִיל בִּצְדָקָה, כּוֹפֶה מֵעָלָיו מַלְאַךְ־הַמָּוֶת, שֶׁאֵינוֹ יָכוֹל לִשְׁלוֹט בּוֹ, וַאֲפִילוּ אִם נִקְנְסָה עָלָיו מִיתָה. וְכֵן הוּא אוֹמֵר, לֹא־יוֹעִילוּ אוֹצְרוֹת רֶשַׁע וּצְדָקָה תַּצִּיל מִמָּוֶת. וְלֹא עוֹד אֶלָּא, שֶׁעוֹמֶדֶת לוֹ לָעוֹלָם־הַבָּא, שֶׁאֵין בּוֹ מָוֶת, שֶׁנֶּאֱמַר, וְדֶרֶךְ נְתִיבָה אַל־מָוֶת.

So great is *tzedakah* that one who does it eats its fruit in this world and the principal remains for him for the World to Come. As it is written: "His *tzedakah* stands forever." [Psalms 112:9] And not only that, but all the acts of *tzedakah* that Jews do for one another, the Holy and Blessed One considers them [the acts] as if they were done for God. As it is written: "Only in God, He said to me, is there victory and might for man." [Isaiah 45:24]

My students, go out and see how great the power of *tzedakah* can be. If a person brings a burnt offering, he only receives the reward for a burnt offering. If he brings a *minchah* offering, he only receives the reward for a *minchah*. If he brings a peace offering [*shelamim*], he only receives the reward for a peace offering. But when a person does *tzedakah*, he receives reward as if he had brought all the sacrifices. As it is written: "Offer the sacrifices of righteousness and trust in God." [Psalms 4:6] The text does not say sacrifice in the singular but rather sacrifices in the plural in order to teach that

גְּדוֹלָה הִיא הַצְּדָקָה, שֶׁהוּא אוֹכֵל הַפֵּרוֹת בָּעוֹלָם־הַזֶּה וְהַקֶּרֶן קַיֶּמֶת לוֹ לָעוֹלָם־הַבָּא, שֶׁנֶּאֱמַר, צִדְקָתוֹ עֹמֶדֶת לָעַד. וְלֹא עוֹד אֶלָּא, כָּל הַצְּדָקוֹת שֶׁעוֹשִׂין יִשְׂרָאֵל זֶה עִם זֶה, הַקָּדוֹשׁ־בָּרוּךְ־הוּא מַחֲשֵׁב לָהֶן כְּאִלּוּ לְפָנָיו הֵן עוֹשִׂין, כָּעִנְיָן שֶׁנֶּאֱמַר, אַךְ בַּיְיָ לִי אָמַר צְדָקוֹת וָעֹז עָדָיו יָבוֹא וְגוֹ'.

בָּנַי, צְאוּ וּרְאוּ כַּמָּה גְדוֹלָה כֹּחָהּ שֶׁל צְדָקָה, אָדָם מֵבִיא עוֹלָה, שְׂכַר עוֹלָה בְּיָדוֹ. מִנְחָה, שְׂכַר מִנְחָה בְּיָדוֹ. שְׁלָמִים, שְׂכַר שְׁלָמִים בְּיָדוֹ. אָדָם עוֹשֶׂה צְדָקָה, שְׂכַר כָּל הַקָּרְבָּנוֹת בְּיָדוֹ, שֶׁנֶּאֱמַר, זִבְחוּ זִבְחֵי־צֶדֶק וּבִטְחוּ אֶל־יְיָ. זֶבַח לֹא נֶאֱמַר אֶלָּא זְבָחֵי, מְלַמֵּד, שֶׁהִיא חֲבִיבָה מִכָּל הַקָּרְבָּנוֹת כֻּלָּן. וְכֵן הוּא אוֹמֵר, הַמִּזְבֵּחַ עֵץ שָׁלוֹשׁ אַמּוֹת וְגוֹ'. וַיְדַבֵּר אֵלַי זֶה הַשֻּׁלְחָן אֲשֶׁר לִפְנֵי יְיָ. פָּתַח בַּמִּזְבֵּחַ וְסִיֵּם בַּשֻּׁלְחָן? אֶלָּא לוֹמַר לָךְ, כָּל זְמַן שֶׁבֵּית־הַמִּקְדָּשׁ קַיָּם, הָיָה הַמִּזְבֵּחַ מְכַפֵּר. מִשֶּׁחָרַב בֵּית־הַמִּקְדָּשׁ, נַעֲשָׂה שֻׁלְחָנוֹ שֶׁל אָדָם מִזְבֵּחַ כַּפָּרָתוֹ.

18

tzedakah is dearer than all of the sacrifices combined. Therefore, the Bible says: "The wooden altar three cubits high and two cubits long was of wood, as were the inner corners, its length, and its walls. And he said to me, 'This is the table that stands before God.'" [Ezekiel 41:22] Why does the verse begin with the altar and conclude with the table? It is to teach you that during the time that the Temple existed, the altar granted atonement. Once the Temple was destroyed, the table of the human being [his deeds] was made into the altar for his atonement.

My students, go out and see how great is the power of *tzedakah*. That when the nations of the world do *tzedakah*, the Holy One ascribes it to them and they receive a reward for it. Behold that Esau, the evil one, merited a kingdom greater than all the other nations and God granted him long reign in the world because he did *tzedakah* for his father when he provided him [Isaac] with food and drink.

בָּנַי, צְאוּ וּרְאוּ כַּמָּה גָדוֹל כֹּחָהּ שֶׁל צְדָקָה. שֶׁאֲפִילוּ אֻמּוֹת־הָעוֹלָם כְּשֶׁעוֹשִׂין צְדָקָה, הַקָּדוֹשׁ־בָּרוּךְ־הוּא תּוֹלֶה לָהֶן וּמְקַבְּלִין עָלֶיהָ שָׂכָר, שֶׁהֲרֵי עֵשָׂו הָרָשָׁע בִּשְׁבִיל שֶׁעָשָׂה צְדָקָה עִם אָבִיו וְהֶאֱכִילוֹ וְהִשְׁקָהוּ, זָכָה לְקַבֵּל מַלְכוּת יוֹתֵר מִכָּל שְׁאָר הָאֻמּוֹת וְנָתַן לוֹ אַרְכָּא לְמַלְכוּתוֹ.

My students, come and see how dear *tzedakah* is before God, that even if *tzedakah* is given unintentionally from a person's money, it is ascribed to him as perfect *tzedakah*.

בָּנַי, בּוֹאוּ וּרְאוּ כַּמָּה חֲבִיבָה הַצְּדָקָה לִפְנֵי הַמָּקוֹם. שֶׁאֲפִילוּ נַעֲשֵׂית צְדָקָה מִמָּמוֹנוֹ שֶׁל אָדָם בְּלֹא מִתְכַּוֵּן, הֲרֵי זוֹ עוֹלָה לוֹ לִצְדָקָה גְמוּרָה.

Therefore, my students, be careful with deeds of *tzedakah*, so that you will exist in quiet, security, and peace in this world and so that you will merit the days of the Messiah and the World to Come. As it is written: "For the work of righteousness is peace and the effect of righteousness is calm and confidence forever." [Isaiah 32:17] May God with great mercy enable us to succeed in this virtue.

לָכֵן בָּנַי, הֱווּ זְהִירִין בְּמַעֲשֵׂה הַצְּדָקָה, כְּדֵי שֶׁתַּעַמְדוּ בְּהַשְׁקֵט וָבֶטַח וּבְשָׁלוֹם בָּעוֹלָם הַזֶּה, וְתִזְכּוּ לִימוֹת הַמָּשִׁיחַ וּלְחַיֵּי הָעוֹלָם הַבָּא, כָּעִנְיָן שֶׁנֶּאֱמַר, וְהָיָה מַעֲשֵׂה הַצְּדָקָה שָׁלוֹם וַעֲבֹדַת הַצְּדָקָה הַשְׁקֵט וָבֶטַח עַד־עוֹלָם. הָאֵל יַצְלִיחֵנוּ בָּהּ בְּרַחֲמָיו הָרַבִּים.

Commentary

One of the best known of all Hebrew words is *tzedakah*. Our children put coins into *tzedakah* boxes in religious schools; we contribute to *tzedakah* appeals from various Jewish charities and causes. The common English translation of this word is "charity," although many parents and teachers have pointed out that the word is more connected, both etymologically and conceptually, to *tzedek*—"justice" or "righteousness." For Yechiel, *tzedakah* is a key spiritual virtue whose benefits transcend the obvious and whose effects go far beyond this world.

Tzedakah is a virtue so great, asserts Yechiel, that it reaches and elevates its possessor to *kisei hakavod*—the "throne of God." Most of us think of *tzedakah* merely as the act of giving money to the poor or those in need. We think of it as a material and physical gesture that has a material and physical result. Yet, as Yechiel makes plain, *tzedakah* affects much more than the material world. As a spiritual virtue that can bring a Jew to God's very throne, *tzedakah* also has great *meta*physical strength and power.

Yechiel cites a verse from Proverbs: "The road of *tzedakah* leads to life." (12:28) Yechiel interprets this verse and thus the relationship between *tzedakah* and life from two distinct vantage points—the spiritual and the physical. With regard to the first, Yechiel claims that anyone who acts with *tzedakah* toward a friend "elevates" that friend by giving the latter's spirit "life." The act of *tzedakah*, therefore, transforms us into *mirror-images* of God, who is also a *somech nofelim*—one who "lifts up the fallen," as we read in the *Amidah* prayer. To lift up a friend who is down, whether financially, mentally, or emotionally, is much more than a material act. It is the catalyst for a person's own spiritual resurrection.

Moreover, anyone who performs acts of *tzedakah* regularly achieves not only personal satisfaction in this world but also merits a share of *Olam Haba*—the "World to Come." Whereas Yechiel's first interpretation of the word "life" in the verse cited above refers to the spiritual life of the person in need who receives *tzedakah*, this second interpretation of the word refers to the eternal life that will be won by the Jew who gives it. With this understanding, "the road of *tzedakah*" does indeed lead to life but to a very particular kind of life—the life of the spirit.

Read in yet another way, the "life" to which the road of *tzedakah* leads is also a physical one. Put simply, by offering *tzedakah* in the form of food to a person who is hungry, the giver of *tzedakah* prevents that person from starving to death. In this context, *tzedakah* is the material means by which human beings sustain and nourish those who are less fortunate by providing them with food, shelter, and clothing. Although there are other ways to uplift those in need (e.g., by giving them a job or putting them through school), the act of keeping a person alive or protecting that person from the cold is *tzedakah* in its most primal manifestation.

Despite the necessity and import of *tzedakah* in the material world, Yechiel ultimately links this virtue to the spiritual world. When a Jew performs an act of *tzedakah* for others, God considers the act as if it had been directed toward heaven. Even though the overt beneficiary of the act is another person, the hidden beneficiary is God, since giving *tzedakah* is acting in obedience to God's will. Like prayer, *tzedakah* should be viewed as a spiritual offering—a replacement for the Temple sacrifices and a gift that God holds even more dear. While the

Temple stood, it was on its altar that human atonement took place. With the Temple gone, it is on our own "tables" that atonement must occur. God judges us finally not by the rites, rituals, and ceremonies that we perform but by the way we treat and interact with other human beings.

The virtue of *tzedakah* is not just a Jewish virtue. Its power and benefits extend to all humanity. Even Jacob's twin brother Esau, who is viewed through the rabbinic lens as the symbol of wickedness and the metaphor for foreign nations, received divine favor and great reward for his act of *tzedakah* toward Isaac when he offered his father food and drink during a time of need. While a person's motivation is important, it is not essential. Even if a person *unintentionally* gives *tzedakah*, the deed is still ascribed to that individual as if it were done "perfectly"—i.e., with deliberate intention. The outward benefit of the act seems to counterbalance, even *purify*, whatever lack of inner impulse or motivation might exist.

TZEDAKAH IN JEWISH PIETISM

The Chasidei Ashkenaz promoted strict religious and spiritual discipline in their members. What is central to their worldview is an unflinching focus on our inner lives. While what we do is important, it is who we *are*—the nature of our spiritual beings—that ultimately defines us in God's eyes. Judah the Pious, perhaps this circle's greatest figure, communicates this idea through his writings on *tzedakah*. In a statement that makes plain Judah's emphasis on internal rather than external action, he writes:

> Give *tzedakah* according to your ability and means: one person [might give] greatly, while another person [might give] only a small amount. What is important is that each of them directs his heart toward heaven.[1]

It is clear that with regard to spiritual merit, inner intention—*kavanah*—outweighs the particular sum of money that a person might give as *tzedakah*. What counts is not the amount that someone gives but the *spirit* in which it is given. The essential requirement for giving *tzedakah* is that its giver direct his or her heart "toward heaven"—i.e., toward God, who directs us to act justly and compassionately. When we give, we should give for God's sake, not our own. Giving is an expression of our subservience to God, not a testimony to our own moral greatness.

Judah goes on to maintain that when "someone who is poor gives only a penny, it is measured against the riches that a wealthy man gives."[2] Judah teaches that we are evaluated by the content of our souls, by our inner impulses and inclinations. God judges us in relation to who we are and not according to our means. The pocket full of change given by a homeless person as *tzedakah* might have more significance to that individual than giving a $100,000 contribution might have to a billionaire. Here again we see that a person's inner life, as opposed to that person's external material means, is the true indicator of an individual's spiritual worth.

A deeper mark of one's inner spirituality becomes apparent when a person puts the interests of others first, ahead of his or her own:

> If a man [already] owns a good house [one that is strong enough], so
> that he does not fear that it will burn down, it is better that he not
> purchase a new house in order that the money he will have saved may
> be used for the purpose of *tzedakah*.[3]

When we encounter a situation that gives us the opportunity to "better" ourselves, we should think twice. For example, the money that the man would have spent to buy a new house is money that he could have used for *tzedakah*. By increasing our own material well-being, we are in effect *decreasing* the ways and means of caring for other, less fortunate human beings. Judah seems to be saying that we should be satisfied with what we already have—at least materially—and use whatever extra resources we might have not to make our own living conditions more luxurious but to give to the hungry and the poor. In this way, the moral impulse, rather than the materialistic one, becomes our guiding principle.

TZEDAKAH IN JEWISH MYSTICISM

Although *tzedakah* may be one of the best known of all Hebrew words and Jewish concepts, it is also one of the most difficult to define. Part of this difficulty lies in the fact that *tzedakah* can be expressed in many ways, with a multiplicity of effects. Rabbi Zaddok ha-Kohen of Lublin, a significant figure in the chasidic movement at the turn of this century, wrote extensively on matters of the soul. For him, the virtue of *tzedakah* is among the most general of all spiritual virtues, serving as a kind of catchall concept for certain basics in Jewish thought and behavior. Zaddok writes:

> *Tzedakah* is commonly referred to as a "generic commandment"
> [*setam mitzvah*], and it appears that that is because it encompasses all
> [the commandments]—for the world came to be as the product of the
> 613 commandments of the Torah.[4]

Zaddok claims that *tzedakah* must be understood less as a specific commandment than as a general rubric or category. In the above statement, *tzedakah* is treated as a spiritual virtue that encompasses all 613 of the Torah's *mitzvot*. But Zaddok goes a step farther. By connecting the world's creation to the mystical force of these commandments, he is also connecting it to a primeval act of *tzedakah*. We should infer, therefore, that God was the agent who, through this first gift of *tzedakah*, set all of reality into motion. Just as one who offers *tzedakah* fills the emptiness of a person in need, so did God fill the dark void that existed before creation.

Despite the fact that *tzedakah* is a "generic commandment," it clearly holds great power. One of its benefits, according to Zaddok, is its ability to correct and purify past sins and transgressions. He writes:

> [Giving] *tzedakah* to the poor can be useful as a corrective for [one's]
> sins…. But only if a person repents properly and asks for the compas-

sion of heaven will God, may He be blessed, repair that person's sins completely.[5]

We have already explained how acts of *tzedakah* can "fill" the empty spaces in our world. Now we are told that this same spiritual virtue can "repair" our souls and "fix" our moral characters. According to the mystics, when we sin, we place our souls in a state of spiritual *brokenness.* Just as Lurianic Kabbalah held that the performance of *mitzvot* would lead to the repair and reunification of the shattered cosmos, so Zaddok posits that the act of *tzedakah* will repair/mend the damage that sin and transgression do to our souls.

There is one qualification. To merely give *tzedakah* is not enough: One must combine the act of giving *tzedakah* with true repentance. Unlike Yechiel, who claims that even someone who gives *tzedakah* unintentionally will receive its full benefits, Zaddok argues that *kavanah*—"inner intention"—is critical to the process as a whole. Without genuine contrition and a heartfelt plea for forgiveness and compassion, God will not "wipe clean" a sinner's misdeeds. Although it may appear that we can use *tzedakah* to compensate for any damage we might have caused, *tzedakah* without proper intention is like a hollow shell and offers little protection to the sinner.

Tzedakah: A Case Study

The virtue of *tzedakah* is attainable by every single Jew, as our thinkers make clear. An enormous number of Jews today, many of whom are uninterested in the rites, rituals, and ceremonies of their religion, give *tzedakah* (sometimes quite generously) to a wide range of causes and foundations, both Jewish and general. For Yechiel, motivation is less important than action; for Zaddok ha-Kohen, *tzedakah* without inner intention is problematic. The following scenario highlights this issue.

THE BENEFACTOR

Cornelius is a young man who recently inherited a great deal of money as a result of his father's death. This inheritance has made it unnecessary for Cornelius to work, and he has spent much of his time of late doing the things that he lacked the time and money for just a short while ago. He is generous with his newly acquired fortune and often treats his friends to gifts or nights on the town. A few weeks ago, Cornelius took his girlfriend Beth on an all-expenses-paid trip to Paris.

On his return and at Beth's suggestion, Cornelius has begun to think about using his wealth for more charitable purposes. His father was active in many causes and always received invitations to the city's most prestigious functions and benefits. Cornelius thinks a donation to Manischewitz Hospital might be the best way to use his funds, since that facility desperately needs a new kidney center. He offers to give the hospital whatever it needs, with two conditions: The center must be named after him, and he must have ultimate control over how his contribution is spent.

— *SHOULD THE HOSPITAL ACCEPT HIS OFFER?* —

QUESTIONS FOR DISCUSSION

1. Does the hospital really face a conflict? What sorts of issues or problems might the administration face as a result of its acceptance of this "gift"?

2. What do you think are some of the factors that motivate this benefactor?

3. Why do you think Cornelius chose to make his donation to this particular hospital? What went into his decision-making process?

4. In what ways might Cornelius's preconditions be ethically or practically problematic? Should the administrators of the hospital spend their time grappling with them? Why or why not?

5. If a motivation is unethical (or nonethical), to what extent should it affect the benefits of an otherwise ethical and desirable outcome?

6. Do you think that it is more ethical to give *tzedakah* anonymously than with public fanfare? Do you think that a selfish motivation can "negate" the merit a person should receive for his or her charitable action? Is it realistic to desire true selflessness from a benefactor?

---

[1] *Otzar Sefer Chasidim, Tzedakah*

[2] Ibid.

[3] Ibid.

[4] *Kitvei Rabbi Zaddok ha-Kohen* (Baltimore, 1992), *Tzedakah*

[5] Ibid.

Tefilah
תְּפִלָּה

Come, my students, and I will teach you about the virtue of prayer. Know, my students, that the virtue of prayer [tefilah] is very dear in the eyes of the Holy One, for the prayers were instituted in place of the sacrifices. As the sages, of blessed memory, said: "The prayers were instituted to correspond to the daily offerings." [Genesis Bereshit Rabbah 68:11] How is this? The daily Shacharit prayer was instituted in place of the daily morning offering. The Minchah prayer was instituted in place of the daily twilight offering. The Ma'ariv prayer was instituted in place of the limbs and the suet that were not consumed while it was still daytime and that were sacrificed and burned on all night. And on any day when there was an extra [musaf] sacrifice, there is a Musaf service. And thus it is written: "Take words with you and return to God. Say to God, 'Forgive all guilt and accept what is good, and we will pay [the offering] with our lips instead of with bulls.'" [Hosea 14:3] And the sages, of blessed memory, said in an aggadah: "Who pays [makes up] for the bulls that we used to offer before You? [We pay with] our lips, with the prayers that we pray before You. For if we need sacrifices, 'Lebanon does not contain fuel enough, nor are there enough beasts for sacrifice' [Isaiah 40:16], because our sins are many. Therefore, we do not have anything to pay in place of the sacrifices except our prayers, which we offer with our lips." [Pesikta de-Rav 165:2]

בָּנַי, בֹּאוּ וַאֲלַמֶּדְכֶם מַעֲלַת הַתְּפִלָּה. דְּעוּ בָּנַי כִּי מַעֲלַת הַתְּפִלָּה, מַעֲלָה יְקָרָה בְּעֵינֵי הַמָּקוֹם־בָּרוּךְ־הוּא, שֶׁהֲרֵי הַתְּפִלּוֹת נִתְקְנוּ בִּמְקוֹם הַקָּרְבָּנוֹת, שֶׁכָּךְ אָמְרוּ חֲכָמֵינוּ זִכְרוֹנָם לִבְרָכָה, תְּפִלּוֹת כְּנֶגֶד תְּמִידִין תִּקְנוּם. כֵּיצַד, תְּפִלַּת שַׁחֲרִית כְּנֶגֶד תָּמִיד שֶׁל שָׁחַר. וּתְפִלַּת הַמִּנְחָה, כְּנֶגֶד תָּמִיד שֶׁל בֵּין־הָעַרְבָּים. וּתְפִלַּת הָעֶרֶב, כְּנֶגֶד אֵבָרִים וּפְדָרִים שֶׁלֹּא נִתְעַכְּלוּ מִבְּעוֹד־יוֹם שֶׁקְּרֵבִין וְהוֹלְכִין כָּל הַלָּיְלָה. וְכָל יוֹם שֶׁיֵּשׁ בּוֹ קָרְבַּן־מוּסָף, יֵשׁ בּוֹ תְּפִלַּת הַמּוּסָפִין. וְכֵן הוּא אוֹמֵר, קְחוּ עִמָּכֶם דְּבָרִים וְשׁוּבוּ אֶל־יְיָ אִמְרוּ אֵלָיו כָּל־תִּשָּׂא עָוֹן וְקַח־טוֹב וּנְשַׁלְּמָה פָרִים שְׂפָתֵינוּ. וְאָמְרוּ חֲכָמֵינוּ זִכְרוֹנָם לִבְרָכָה בָּאַגָּדָה, מִי מְשַׁלֵּם אוֹתָם הַפָּרִים שֶׁהָיִינוּ מַקְרִיבִים לְפָנֶיךָ? שְׂפָתֵינוּ, בַּתְּפִלָּה שֶׁאָנוּ מִתְפַּלְלִין לְפָנֶיךָ. שֶׁאִם לַקָּרְבָּנוֹת אָנוּ צְרִיכִין – וּלְבָנוֹן אֵין דֵּי בָעֵר וְחַיָּתוֹ אֵין דֵּי עוֹלָה. לְפִי שֶׁחֲטָאתֵינוּ מְרֻבִּין. לְפִיכָךְ, אֵין לָנוּ לְשַׁלֵּם בִּמְקוֹם הַקָּרְבָּנוֹת אֶלָּא תְּפִלּוֹתֵינוּ שֶׁאָנוּ מְנִיבִין בִּשְׂפָתוֹתֵינוּ.

Great is the power of prayer. Every time that a person prays and directs his heart to God in the heavens [*Aviv shebashamayim*], the Holy One receives the prayer. And not only that, but God pardons all of his iniquities. As it is written: "For You are not a God who desires wickedness; evil cannot abide with You." [Psalms 5:5]

גָּדוֹל כֹּחָהּ שֶׁל תְּפִלָּה. שֶׁכָּל זְמַן שֶׁאָדָם מִתְפַּלֵּל וּמְכַוֵּן לִבּוֹ לְאָבִיו שֶׁבַּשָּׁמַיִם, הַקָּדוֹשׁ־בָּרוּךְ־הוּא מְקַבֵּל תְּפִלָּתוֹ. וְלֹא עוֹד אֶלָּא שֶׁמּוֹחֵל לוֹ עַל כָּל עֲוֹנוֹתָיו, שֶׁנֶּאֱמַר, כִּי לֹא אֵל חָפֵץ רֶשַׁע, אָתָּה, לֹא יְגֻרְךָ רָע.

My students, do not take prayer [services] lightly, because the patriarchs themselves instituted them. Thus the sages, of blessed memory, say in an *aggadah* [*Proverbs Rabbah* 22:28]: What is the meaning of what is written, "Do not remove the ancient boundary stone that your ancestors set up"? [Proverbs 22:28] If you see a custom that your ancestors practiced, do not change it. For example, Abraham instituted the morning service. As it is written: "Abraham arose early and hurried to the place where he stood [*amad*] before God." [Genesis 19:27] *Amidah* is the same as *tefilah*. As it is written: *Vaya'amod Pinchas vayefalel*—"And Pinchas stood up and intervened [prayed]." [Psalms 106:30] Isaac instituted the *Minchah* service. As it is written: "Isaac went out to meditate [*lasu'ach*] in the field toward evening." [Genesis 24:63] What is meditation [*sichah*] if not prayer? As it is written: "A prayer of a lowly man when he wraps himself and pours forth his plea [*sicho*] before God." [Psalms 102:1] Jacob instituted the evening service. As it is written: "He came upon [*vayifga*] the place and stopped there for the night, for the sun had set." [Genesis 28:11] What is "stopping/alighting/touching" [*pegiah*] if not prayer? As it is written: "Let them intercede [*yifge'u*] with the God of hosts." [Jeremiah 27:18] And do not say, "Now I will institute

בָּנַי, אַל תְּהִי הַתְּפִלָּה קַלָּה בְּעֵינֵיכֶם, מִפְּנֵי שֶׁהַתְּפִלּוֹת אֲבוֹת־הָעוֹלָם תִּקְּנוּם. שֶׁכָּךְ אָמְרוּ חֲכָמֵינוּ זִכְרוֹנָם לִבְרָכָה בָּאַגָּדָה, מַאי דִכְתִיב, אַל־תַּסֵּג גְּבוּל עוֹלָם אֲשֶׁר עָשׂוּ אֲבוֹתֶיךָ. אִם רָאִיתָ מִנְהָג שֶׁעָשׂוּ אֲבוֹתֶיךָ, אַל תְּשַׁנֶּה אוֹתוֹ. כְּגוֹן אַבְרָהָם שֶׁתִּקֵּן תְּפִלַּת שַׁחֲרִית, שֶׁנֶּאֱמַר, וַיַּשְׁכֵּם אַבְרָהָם בַּבֹּקֶר אֶל־הַמָּקוֹם אֲשֶׁר־עָמַד שָׁם וְגוֹ'. וְאֵין עֲמִידָה אֶלָּא תְּפִלָּה, שֶׁנֶּאֱמַר, וַיַּעֲמֹד פִּינְחָס וַיְפַלֵּל. יִצְחָק תִּקֵּן תְּפִלַּת הַמִּנְחָה, שֶׁנֶּאֱמַר, וַיֵּצֵא יִצְחָק לָשׂוּחַ בַּשָּׂדֶה לִפְנוֹת עָרֶב. וְאֵין שִׂיחָה אֶלָּא תְּפִלָּה, שֶׁנֶּאֱמַר, תְּפִלָּה לְעָנִי כִי־יַעֲטֹף וְלִפְנֵי יְיָ יִשְׁפֹּךְ שִׂיחוֹ. יַעֲקֹב תִּקֵּן תְּפִלַּת עַרְבִית, שֶׁנֶּאֱמַר, וַיִּפְגַּע בַּמָּקוֹם וַיָּלֶן שָׁם כִּי־בָא הַשָּׁמֶשׁ. וְאֵין פְּגִיעָה אֶלָּא תְּפִלָּה, שֶׁנֶּאֱמַר, יִפְגְּעוּ־נָא בַּיָי צְבָאוֹת. וְלֹא תֹאמַר, אַף אֲנִי אֲתַקֵּן תְּפִלָּה אַחֶרֶת, תַּלְמוּד לוֹמַר, אֲשֶׁר עָשׂוּ אֲבוֹתֶיךָ. וְלֹא עֲשָׂאוּהָ לָהֶם בִּלְבַד, אֶלָּא לְכָל הַדּוֹרוֹת עֲשָׂאוּהָ. וְכֵן מְפֹרָשׁ עַל יְדֵי דָוִד עָלָיו הַשָּׁלוֹם, עֶרֶב וָבֹקֶר וְצָהֳרַיִם אָשִׂיחָה וְאֶהֱמֶה וַיִּשְׁמַע קוֹלִי.

27

another prayer service," for the Torah teaches: "Do not remove the ancient boundary stone that your ancestors set up." [Proverbs 22:28] And they did not establish it for themselves only, but rather they did it for all the generations. And thus it is explained by David, may he rest in peace: "Evening, morning, and noon, I will mediate [*asichah*] and moan, and God will hear my voice." [Psalms 55:18]

And the sages, of blessed memory, said: "The one who prays should direct his eyes downward, lest he will look here and there and turn his heart to another place. And he should direct his heart upward in order that he will concentrate on the prayer." [*Berachot* 28:2]

וְאָמְרוּ חֲכָמֵינוּ זִכְרוֹנָם לִבְרָכָה, הַמִּתְפַּלֵּל, צָרִיךְ שֶׁיִּתֵּן עֵינָיו לְמַטָּה, כְּדֵי שֶׁלֹּא יִסְתַּכֵּל לְכָאן וּלְכָאן וְיִפְנֶה לִבּוֹ בְּמָקוֹם אַחֵר, וִיכַוֵּן לִבּוֹ לְמַעְלָה, כְּדֵי שֶׁיְּהֵא מְכַוֵּן לִבּוֹ בַּתְּפִלָּה.

And everyone who rises early and stays up late in order to be able to pray in the synagogue [with the community] is considered to have gone out to greet God [*Shechinah*]. As it is written: "The righteous shall surely praise Your name; the upright shall dwell in Your presence." [Psalms 140:14]

וְכָל הַמַּשְׁכִּים וּמַעֲרִיב לְהִתְפַּלֵּל בְּבֵית־הַכְּנֶסֶת, כְּאִלּוּ מְקַבֵּל פְּנֵי־שְׁכִינָה, שֶׁנֶּאֱמַר, אַךְ צַדִּיקִים יוֹדוּ לִשְׁמֶךָ יֵשְׁבוּ יְשָׁרִים אֶת־פָּנֶיךָ.

Therefore, my students, since the Holy One desires the prayers of Israel and desires them even more when one prays in the synagogue with the community [*tzibur*], when you arise from your beds, be careful and diligent to cleanse yourselves from all impurity and dirt, and go to the synagogue and turn

לָכֵן בָּנַי, הוֹאִיל שֶׁהַקָּדוֹשׁ־בָּרוּךְ־הוּא חָפֵץ בְּתִפְלוֹתֵיהֶן שֶׁל יִשְׂרָאֵל וּבְיוֹתֵר מִי שֶׁמִּתְפַּלֵּל בְּבָתֵּי־כְּנֵסִיּוֹת עִם הַצִּבּוּר – כְּשֶׁתָּקוּמוּ מִמִּטּוֹתֵיכֶם, הֱווּ זְהִירִין וּזְרִיזִין לְנַקּוֹת אֶת עַצְמְכֶם מִכָּל טֻמְאָה וְטִנּוּף, וְתֵלְכוּ לְבֵית־הַכְּנֶסֶת וְתִפְנוּ לִבְּכֶם מִכָּל

your hearts from all other matters and business and the other vanities of the world in order that your thoughts will not disturb you and confuse you in your prayer.

And try to pray all your prayers in their right time and in their right order; and read the *Shema* in the morning and evening at the right time so that the Holy One will receive your prayers willingly and you will merit the opportunity to see the building of the Temple. As it is written, "And I will bring them to My sacred mount, and I will make them able to rejoice in My house of prayer. Their burnt offerings shall be welcome on My alter; for My house shall be called a house of prayer for all peoples." [Isaiah 56:7]

שְׁאָר הָעִנְיָנִים וְהָעֲסָקִים וּשְׁאָר הַבְלֵי־הָעוֹלָם, כְּדֵי שֶׁלֹּא יַטְרִידוּ אֶתְכֶם הַמַּחֲשָׁבוֹת וִיבַלְבְּלוּ אֶתְכֶם בִּתְפִלַּתְכֶם. וְהִשְׁתַּדְּלוּ לְהִתְפַּלֵּל כָּל תְּפִלּוֹתֵיכֶם בְּעוֹנָתָן וְסִדְרָן, וְתִקְרְאוּ קְרִיַת־שְׁמַע שַׁחֲרִית וְעַרְבִית בְּעוֹנָתָה, כְּדֵי שֶׁיְּקַבֵּל הַקָּדוֹשׁ־בָּרוּךְ־הוּא תְּפִלּוֹתֵיכֶם לְרָצוֹן, וְתִזְכּוּ לִרְאוֹת בְּבִנְיָן בֵּית־הַמִּקְדָּשׁ, כָּעִנְיָן שֶׁנֶּאֱמַר, וַהֲבִיאוֹתִים אֶל־הַר קָדְשִׁי וְשִׂמַּחְתִּים בְּבֵית תְּפִלָּתִי עוֹלֹתֵיהֶם וְזִבְחֵיהֶם לְרָצוֹן עַל־מִזְבְּחִי כִּי בֵיתִי בֵּית־תְּפִלָּה יִקָּרֵא לְכָל־הָעַמִּים.

Commentary

The necessity for *tefilah*—"prayer"—is one of the major tenets of Judaism. According to Jewish tradition, a Jew is obliged to pray three times daily at fixed times and with a prescribed liturgy, the *siddur*. While a great number of prayers are private in nature, others have a more collective thrust. Some of the prayers are songs of praise for God; others are prayers of petition for health, peace, forgiveness, etc.; still others, like the *Shema Yisrael*, are statements of creed/belief. Even though there are many different types and forms of prayers, Yechiel sees in all of them the same underlying foundation. As he points out, the origin and importance of *tefilah* is related directly to the end of the practice of sacrifice, which came about with the Temple's destruction by the Romans in 70 C.E.. The prayers, notes Yechiel, were fixed in place of and to correspond to the Temple sacrifices: The morning service, *Shacharit*, replaces the morning offering; the afternoon service, *Minchah*, relates to the twilight offering; and the evening service, *Ma'ariv*, substitutes for the evening offering. Moreover, just as some holy days require an extra sacrifice—*musaf*—so on certain days (e.g., on Shabbat), does our liturgy require an extra service.

While Jews were able to worship God and pay for their sins through the sacrifice of pigeons and bulls during the time that the Temple stood, post-Temple Judaism dictates that we must offer divine service in an alternative way. The destruction of the Second Temple forced the replacement of animal sacrifice with prayer. From that time on, rather than serving God through physical objects, Jews have shown reverence for God through the use of *words*. The *Amidah* begins, "O God, open my lips that my mouth may declare Your praise." Thus what a

Jew *feels*, what a Jew *expresses*, is now at least as important as what he or she *does*.

Yechiel implies that there is a direct correlation between the intent—*kavanah*—in a Jew's heart and mind when he or she prays and the divine acceptance of that prayer. If an individual concentrates when he or she prays and directs his or her thoughts, feelings, and soul toward God, the Holy One will respond by accepting that person's prayers. Inner intention, not outer action, plays the key role in the spiritual dynamics of prayer. In addition, God will pardon a person of all his or her iniquities. Here, the concept of *tefilah* operates much like that of *teshuvah* in that a sound spiritual attitude holds the power to erase all previous bad intentions and actions.

The liturgy must be treated with great reverence, Yechiel maintains, because it was the patriarchs themselves who put it in place. As Proverbs teaches us, if a custom has been established by one's ancestors, one is not at liberty to change it. But how does Yechiel know that it was the patriarchs who fixed our service structure? Although the Torah offers no *overt* mention of the traditional Jewish prayers, Yechiel finds them beneath the surface, the result of biblical exegesis.

Abraham's actions suggest that it was he who initiated the daily Jewish prayer cycle with the world's first *Shacharit* "service"; Isaac followed with *Minchah* at dusk, and Jacob fixed *Ma'ariv* after the sun had set, at night. Just as the father-son-grandson chain extends over the course of a lifetime, so does the morning-afternoon-evening prayer cycle extend over the course of a single day. We may not alter this structure, Yechiel maintains, because it was not established exclusively for us. Rather, it was created for *all* generations. In this way, the Jewish prayers serve to unite past, present, and future in a single, unbroken totality.

Prayer requires complete concentration. In order to minimize the threat of potential distractions, Yechiel advocates that a Jew engaged in prayer must direct his or her eyes downward, toward the earth, lest he or she "will look here and there" and turn his or her focus and attention "to another place" (e.g., to greet friends, to admire someone's appearance, etc.). During *tefilah* the concerns of the world must be driven from the Jew's consciousness. Instead, a person must direct his or her concentration upward, toward the heavens, that region beyond the pull of human need and above the constraints of matter and form.

When Jews pray in the synagogue as a community, it is as if they stand with the Divine Presence, the *Shechinah*. In Yechiel's view, God desires the prayers of the people of Israel but desires them even more when they are offered *collectively* by the people of Israel as a community. While private prayer is important, public prayer is superior. The spirituality of prayer thus becomes inextricably linked to the concept of a *tzibur*—a "community" that is bound together by faith and by destiny. Perhaps this helps to explain why after nearly two millennia, the synagogue still remains *the* central Jewish institution.

The virtue of *tefilah* is connected to the Messianic Days. If a Jew offers all his or her prayers "in their right time and in their right order"—i.e., according to Jewish tradition—that Jew will merit a vision of the Temple rebuilt. At the end of days, when the Temple stands once again, the act of divine service will come around full circle: The "burnt offerings" of the people of Israel will be welcome in God's "house of prayer," although the exact nature of those offerings—i.e., whether they are verbal or animal—is unclear.

TEFILAH IN JEWISH PIETISM

Bachya ibn Pakuda wrote his masterpiece *Hovot ha-Levavot*, "Duties of the Heart," in eleventh-century Spain. It became one of the most influential and lasting books in all of Jewish pietistic literature. In its chapter on "Spiritual Accounting," Bachya grapples with the issue of prayer. Since the stated purpose of Bachya's book is to explore the inner duties and dynamics of the soul, it is not surprising that Bachya's primary approach to the topic of *tefilah* is through a discussion of the Jew's spiritual quest for self-examination. After having cleansed himself or herself from all external distractions and extraneous thoughts, the Jew at prayer

> should take to heart who it is to whom he intends to offer this prayer, what he seeks therein, and how he is to address his Maker both as to choice of words and of theme. For know that words are uttered with the tongue and are like a shell, while meditation on the words is in the heart and is the kernel. Words are the body of prayer, and meditation on their meaning is the spirit. If a person prays with his tongue and his heart is otherwise engaged, his prayer is like a body without a spirit or a shell without a kernel, because his body is present but his heart is not with him while he is praying.[1]

The words "Know before whom you stand" often appear over the ark that a Jew faces in the synagogue. Bachya uses that phrase to convey the idea that before a Jew engages in prayer, he or she must first become aware of the true object of those prayers, as well as the prayers' goals and presentation. Since the "object" of *tefilah* is none other than the living God, a Jew must pray as if he or she were standing in the presence of a great and mighty king and must exhibit the reverence and humility that such an encounter warrants.

The words of prayer, writes Bachya, are like the shell of a nut, while the essence of their meaning is like a nut's kernel. The act of praying is a physical act: One's lips and tongue move, the vocal cords reverberate, the throat emits a sound. The *cognition* of those words, however, is a spiritual cognition and, therefore, occurs in the heart. Without this inner grasp of the import and meaning of prayers, our prayers are like an empty husk, a body without a spirit. Authentic *tefilah* goes beyond mere mechanics and fuses the physical and the spiritual.

Because the human mind is not always stable and is easily distracted, it would be impossible for individual Jews to arrange the rubrics of prayer for themselves. The sages, therefore, composed the Jewish liturgy in its proper sequence and structure as a guide to future generations. The *siddur* thus houses the "shells" of our early sages' spiritual aspirations, and it is up to each individual generation to provide these shells with a contemporary soul.

Bachya writes:

> Our devotion in prayer is nothing but the soul's longing for God, humbling itself in His presence, exalting its Creator, offering praises and thanksgiving to His name, casting all its burdens upon Him....
> Words need a subject [of thought] but a subject of thought is not in

need of speech if it is possible to set it in orderly fashion in the heart. The latter is the essence of our devotion and the chief aim to which our attention should be directed.[2]

In the end, *tefilah* is the soul's expression of its longing for God, its desire to reunite with its Source. God does not "need" words. It is our words that require a God. The words of prayer thus mediate between the divine and the human and represent the signs of our distance from God and the immediate, unfiltered experience of the Holy. The true essence of our devotion, then—and the principal goal toward which our efforts must strive—*transcends* language: It is the expression of the heart's silent, hidden, internal yearning for God.

TEFILAH IN JEWISH MYSTICISM

Rabbi Dov Baer, the Maggid of Mezhirech, deals at great length in his writings with the concept of *tefilah*. For him, as for many other chasidic thinkers, prayer at its most profound level must be understood in a purely contemplative mode. Rather than asking for things, praising, thanking, or stating beliefs, the Jew engaged in contemplative prayer has a more mystical agenda: the ecstatic experience of union with God called *devekut*. Dov Baer writes:

> This is the meaning of "Happy is the king who is praised in his house" [Babylonian Talmud, *Berachot* 3a]—that the body becomes the house of the Holy One, blessed be He, for [the Chasid] must pray with all his strength until he bursts out of his material nature and forgets his own self, so that only the vitality that is in God remains, and all his thoughts are directed to Him. [In this state of ecstasy] he will not even be aware of the intensity of his prayer, for if he is, he will remember himself....[3]

When the Chasid prays with abandon, with all of his or her energy and strength, a transformation occurs: The Chasid literally "loses" himself or herself. In the throes of spiritual rapture, which contemplative prayer can induce, the Chasid loses touch with his or her own senses, forgets not only where he or she is but also *who* he or she is. With the loss of self-consciousness and the negation of any sense of ego, the Chasid can mystically transcend his or her material condition.

After the Chasid's body has thus been "vacated" of its (psychic) contents, it may then become a proper vessel, or "house," for God's presence. As the Chasid's sense of self is destroyed, so, too, is the illusion that he or she has any independent reality apart from God. This notion is consistent with much of the more radical or "quietistic" streams in Western mystical thought, in which distinctions between God, self, and world tend to disappear when one attains the level of mystical insight.

The experience of mystical ecstasy, the state in which the mind transcends its ordinary limitations, does not necessarily entail outwardly visible manifestations:

Sometimes a man is able to pray in love, fear, and great enthusiasm
without any [external] movement.... [In this condition] he may serve
God with his soul alone,...which is a better and more effective way
to pray to God, may He be blessed, than the prayer that is visible
externally through his limbs.[4]

Once the Chasid has reached the higher levels of prayer and meditation, it matters little
whether he or she speaks or is silent, although the latter is the favored mode of spiritual
expression. If there is speech, then it is "automatic" speech or the Divine Presence, the
Shechinah, speaking *through* the Chasid. If he or she is silent, then the Chasid serves God
through his or her soul alone, and the only movement is the motion of his or her thoughts.
The Maggid writes elsewhere that nonverbal prayer is, in fact, the proper way to respond to
the "fire of silence" that burns within the mystic. As a result of its presence, the mystic will
"cry out in silence" from the passion to serve his or her Creator.

Tefilah: A Case Study

The struggle with *tefilah* is as much a contemporary issue as it was an ancient one. Prayer
has been regarded as one of the central elements of spiritual expression since the dawn of organized religion. The issue of taking time out from our everyday lives to offer formal "prayer"—
whether it be to give thanks or to ask for rain—predates modernity. Since mainstream
religion has grown less and less popular in the latter half of this century, it should come as no
surprise that modern Jews face the same dilemma.

THE SKEPTIC

*Judd is a single, thirty-year-old therapist who lives in New York City. He has had many years
of higher education at the best schools and he has earned a Ph.D. in psychology. After gradu-
ating from college, he spent a year traveling around the world. He is well-read, subscribes to
the Philharmonic, and visits art museums on the weekends. He thinks of himself as a cultured,
liberal, and open-minded person, always willing to hear a new idea or try a new experience.*

*Judd was raised in a Jewish household but considers himself more "spiritual" than Jewish. He
dislikes "organized religion" and feels its formal rituals and rites do more to harm the spirit than
help it. He hated the synagogue in which he grew up and found its rabbi uninspiring and unap-
proachable. Judd derives spiritual uplift from hiking and the meditation courses he takes. Judd's
friend Jill has asked him to join her for a Shabbat service at her synagogue, which she says is
wonderful. Everyone participates in the prayers and songs, and there is a strong sense of community. Judd is skeptical.*

———————— *SHOULD JUDD JOIN JILL?* ————————

Questions for Discussion

1. What exactly is Judd's conflict? How much of it is philosophical and how much of it is emotional?

2. What do you think are some of the barriers that Judd must overcome if he is to feel more comfortable in a synagogue setting?

3. Judd's approach to spirituality has been largely private (hikes and meditation). How might the atmosphere in a synagogue affect that approach?

4. Should Judd feel obligated to accompany Jill to the service because she is his friend? Are there other factors that might lead him to the synagogue?

5. Can a public environment sometimes be more conducive to prayer than a private one? Explain.

6. Why do you think that traditional Judaism favored a fixed, communitarian approach to prayer over a spontaneous, private one? How might the focus on individual rather than corporate expression (e.g., mysticism) erode the structures and authority of religious institutions?

---

[1] *Hovot ha-Levavot* (Jerusalem, 1962), vol. 2, pp. 207-209
[2] Ibid., p. 211
[3] *Or ha-Emet* (Brooklyn, 1960), pp. 4-5
[4] *Likutim Yekarim* (Jerusalem, 1974), p. 63a

Boshet

בּשֶׁת

Come, my students, and I will teach you about the virtue of [avoiding] shame. Know, my students, that the virtue of [avoiding] shame [boshet] is very important because everybody who exhibits shame-facedness/modesty [boshet panim] is rescued from sin and iniquity. As it is written: "Moses said to the people, 'Do not be afraid, because God has come to test you so that the fear of God will be on your faces, lest you sin.'" [Exodus 20:17] And our sages, of blessed memory, said: "So that the fear of God will be on your faces" means embarrassment [bushah]. "Lest you sin" teaches that bushah leads to the fear/avoidance of sin. Therefore, they said, it is a good sign if a person is easily embarrassed [a bayshan].

בָּנַי, בּאוּ וַאֲלַמֶּדְכֶם מַעֲלַת הַבּשֶׁת. דְּעוּ בָנַי, כִּי מַעֲלַת מִדַּת הַבּשֶׁת, מַעֲלָה חֲשׁוּבָה עַד־מְאֹד. שֶׁכָּל מִי שֶׁיֵּשׁ לוֹ בּשֶׁת־פָּנִים, נִצּוֹל מִן הַחֲטָאִים וְהָעֲוֹנוֹת, כְּעִנְיָן שֶׁנֶּאֱמַר, וַיֹּאמֶר משֶׁה אֶל־הָעָם אַל־תִּירָאוּ כִּי לְבַעֲבוּר נַסּוֹת אֶתְכֶם בָּא הָאֱלֹהִים וּבַעֲבוּר תִּהְיֶה יִרְאָתוֹ עַל־פְּנֵיכֶם לְבִלְתִּי תֶחֱטָאוּ. וְאָמְרוּ חֲכָמֵינוּ זִכְרוֹנָם לִבְרָכָה, בַּעֲבוּר תִּהְיֶה יִרְאָתוֹ עַל־פְּנֵיכֶם, זוֹ בּוּשָׁה. לְבִלְתִּי תֶחֱטָאוּ, מְלַמֵּד, שֶׁהַבּוּשָׁה מְבִיאָה לִידֵי יִרְאַת־חֵטְא. מִכָּאן אָמְרוּ, סִימָן יָפֶה לָאָדָם שֶׁיְּהֵא בַּיְשָׁן.

My students, come and see how great this virtue of boshet is before God. Even if a person commits several transgressions and is ashamed of them but does not change them, God pardons all his iniquities. As it is written in Ezekiel 16:63: "Thus you shall remember and feel shame, and you shall be too abashed to open your mouth again, when I have forgiven you for all that you did, declares God."

בָּנַי, בּאוּ וּרְאוּ כַּמָּה גְדוֹלָה מַעֲלַת הַבּשֶׁת לִפְנֵי הַמָּקוֹם. שֶׁאֲפִילוּ עָבַר אָדָם כַּמָּה עֲבֵרוֹת וּמִתְבַּיֵּשׁ מֵהֶן וְאֵינוֹ שׁוֹנֶה בָהֶן, הַקָּדוֹשׁ־בָּרוּךְ־הוּא מוֹחֵל לוֹ עַל כָּל עֲוֹנוֹתָיו, כְּעִנְיָן שֶׁנֶּאֱמַר, לְמַעַן תִּזְכְּרִי וָבשְׁתְּ וְלֹא יִהְיֶה־לָּךְ עוֹד פִּתְחוֹן פֶּה מִפְּנֵי כְּלִמָּתֵךְ בְּכַפְּרִי־לָךְ לְכָל־אֲשֶׁר עָשִׂית נְאֻם אֲדֹנָי אֱלֹהִים.

35

My students, take care not to bring shame to your friends—privately and even more so in public—because this is one of the most severe transgressions that is in the Torah. Thus said our sages, of blessed memory: "Whoever whitens the face of his friend/colleague in public, it is as if he spilled the other's blood, because we see that the blood goes from his face and he becomes pale." [*Baba Metzia* 58b] Further, they said: "Whoever shames his friend will ultimately be shamed himself." [*Masechet Kallah*] And not only that, but the ministering angels will knock him down and display his degradation/indignity to the whole world. They said further: "Everyone who descends to *gehinom* [a place of misery] descends and later ascends—except for three types who descend, never to ascend: the one who commits adultery, the one who calls his neighbor a bad name, and the one who whitens the face of another in public." [*Baba Metzia* 58b]

בָּנֵי, הֱווּ זְהִירִין שֶׁלֹּא לְבַיֵּשׁ פְּנֵי חַבְרֵיכֶם אֲפִילּוּ בֵּינְכֶם לְבֵינָם, וְכָל-שֶׁכֵּן שֶׁלֹּא לְבַיְּשָׁם בָּרַבִּים, מִפְּנֵי שֶׁהִיא מִן הָעֲבֵרוֹת הַחֲמוּרוֹת שֶׁבַּתּוֹרָה. שֶׁכָּךְ אָמְרוּ חֲכָמֵינוּ זִכְרוֹנָם לִבְרָכָה, כָּל הַמַּלְבִּין פְּנֵי חֲבֵרוֹ בָּרַבִּים, כְּאִלּוּ שׁוֹפֵךְ דָּמִים, דְּחָזֵינָא לֵהּ דְּאָזִיל סֻמְקָא וְאָתֵי חִוָּרָא. וְעוֹד אָמְרוּ, כָּל הַמַּבְיֵּשׁ אֶת חֲבֵרוֹ, סוֹפוֹ מִתְבַּיֵּשׁ. וְלֹא עוֹד אֶלָּא שֶׁמַּלְאֲכֵי-הַשָּׁרֵת דּוֹחֲפִין אוֹתוֹ וּמַרְאִין קְלוֹנוֹ לְכָל בָּאֵי-עוֹלָם. וְעוֹד אָמְרוּ, כָּל הַיּוֹרְדִין לְגֵיהִנָּם, יוֹרְדִין וְעוֹלִין, חוּץ מִשְּׁלֹשָׁה שֶׁיּוֹרְדִין וְאֵינָן עוֹלִין, וְאֵלּוּ הֵן. הַבָּא עַל אֵשֶׁת-אִישׁ, וְהַמְכַנֶּה שֵׁם [רַע] לַחֲבֵרוֹ, וְהַמַּלְבִּין פְּנֵי חֲבֵרוֹ בָּרַבִּים.

And what is insolence [*azut*—the opposite of *bushah*]? One who commits a transgression in the presence of others and is not ashamed is called insolent, as is one who repeatedly transgresses the same sin. And one who stands tall and arrogant with his head up and is not ashamed in front of others is the opposite of *bushah*. Such a person who is arrogant and feels no shame in front of others is like an idol worshiper. As it is written in Jeremiah 6:15: "They have acted shamefully; they have done abhorrent things [idol worship]. Yet they do not feel shame, and they cannot be made to blush. Therefore, they shall fall among the falling. They shall stumble when I punish them, said God." And it is said that the result of

וּמַהוּ הָעַזּוּת? שֶׁעוֹבֵר עֲבֵרָה בִּפְנֵי בְּנֵי-אָדָם וְאֵינוֹ מִתְבַּיֵּשׁ מֵהֶן, נִקְרָא עַז-פָּנִים. וְהָעוֹבֵר עֲבֵרָה וְשָׁנָה בָהּ. וְהַהוֹלֵךְ בְּקוֹמָה זְקוּפָה וּבְעַזּוּת-מֵצַח וְאֵינוֹ מִתְבַּיֵּשׁ מִן הָאֲנָשִׁים. שֶׁכָּל מִי שֶׁיֵּשׁ בּוֹ עַזּוּת-פָּנִים וְאֵינוֹ מִתְבַּיֵּשׁ, הֲרֵי הוּא כְּעוֹבֵד עֲבוֹדָה-זָרָה, כָּעִנְיָן שֶׁנֶּאֱמַר, הוֹבִישׁוּ כִּי-תוֹעֵבָה עָשׂוּ גַּם-בּוֹשׁ לֹא-יֵבוֹשׁוּ גַּם-הַכְלִים לֹא יָדָעוּ לָכֵן יִפְּלוּ בַנֹּפְלִים בְּעֵת-פְּקַדְתִּים יִכָּשְׁלוּ אָמַר יְיָ. וְאוֹמֵר, אַחֲרִית הָעַזּוּת, מַחֲלֹקֶת. וְאַחֲרִית הַמַּחֲלֹקֶת, חֲרָטָה.

insolence is controversy/disagreement and
disharmony. And the result of disagreement
is remorse and regret.

[Datan and Aviram suffered from *azut*.]

Commentary

It might seem odd to many of us to think that a concept like shame could have a positive
value. Yet that is precisely Yechiel's claim, namely, that the virtue of *boshet*—"shame"—is of
critical import to the moral and spiritual life of a Jew. Yechiel begins describing the merits of
this key concept by discussing its utilitarian value.

After the revelation of God and the giving of the Ten Commandments at Mount Sinai, the
Children of Israel are in a state of shock. Amidst "the thunder, and the lightning, and the
sound of the *shofar*" (Exodus 20:15) that accompany God's appearance, a list of rules is thrust
upon them. They are intimidated by God and are frightened by this moral burden.

Moses reassures them. By putting the fear of God on their "faces," he argues, they will not
stray from the Law. Yechiel uses this episode as a paradigm for the perennial struggle to be
good—for the conflict we constantly feel between following God's will and being tempted to
do the very opposite.

Yechiel connects the virtue of shame to the fear of God and posits that the former is the
stepping-stone to the latter. One who possesses *boshet panim*—"shamefacedness"—will ultimately be saved from the clutches of sin. In other words, the virtue of *boshet* (as a catalyst for
the fear of God) has a clear utility: It is humanity's shield from temptation, our weapon against
moral transgression.

Yet *boshet* has more than a merely utilitarian value. It is also a value in itself. Yechiel argues that God shows compassion for a person who is ashamed of his or her moral failings, even if he or she repeats those same transgressions. Because it relates to inner attitude as much as to outer behavior, shame is of tremendous *spiritual* worth. *Boshet* reveals the state of one's soul, even when one's body is not quite strong enough to keep up with it.

After having examined the positive aspects of *boshet*, Yechiel turns to the virtue's dark side—its misuse and corruptive quality. He warns us that bringing shame upon our friends, especially if such an act occurs in public, is among the most severe transgressions in the Torah. At its best, *boshet* leads one to reverence and humility. At its worst, it leads one to disgrace and humiliation. It is the context in which one experiences shame that determines its worth.

To shame one's friend in a public situation is akin to spilling that person's blood. It is an attack of the most brutal type, a kind of emotional and psychological *murder*. It is not the victim's body that is assaulted but his or her heart and mind, and these wounds take longer to heal than physical ones, if they heal at all. In the end, however, it is the perpetrator and not the victim who must face the gravest consequences: in this life, degradation before the world; in the next life, spiritual damnation.

In order to better grasp the importance of *boshet*, Yechiel presents us with its opposite, *azut*—"insolence." What is *azut*? It is committing acts of sin before others without care or concern—and without shame. The arrogance of one who is insolent before others by thinking that he or she is "above" them or their rules severs that person from the rest of humanity. Such a person becomes an idolator because while *boshet* leads to reverence for God, *azut*—"lack of shame"—leads to the idolization of self. The result of such self-deification is a fragmented relationship with God and the rest of the world.

BOSHET IN JEWISH PIETISM

In the writings of Judah the Pious, who was introduced in Chapter 2, the concept of *boshet* is of major importance. Like Yechiel, Judah acknowledges that the notion of shame has both positive and negative aspects. He first accentuates the positive: "If one is diligent [with regard to] Torah, *mitzvot*, and good deeds from the time of youth, it becomes difficult to separate oneself from them later on because of shame."[1] The person who has made Jewish observance—Torah study, performance of the *mitzvot*, and ethical behavior—a permanent fixture in his or her life from the very outset will develop a reverence for Jewish observance and an adherence to it that will prevent laxity in the future.

Judah also writes that "one who has committed a sin but demonstrates shame over it is pardoned for all one's [other] sins."[2] This message is similar to Yechiel's: Not only does God have compassion for the person who shows shame over a sinful act, God actually pardons that person for all *other* sins as well. Moreover, Judah claims that "if God had not created *boshet*, a human being could never be cleansed of sin."[3] Shame was created by God to purify us from moral transgression. Without it, we would live in a permanent state of sin, which is a theological position that is at odds with the basic principles of Jewish belief.

Yet *boshet* also has negative aspects. Judah presents us with one such example:

It is forbidden to be seen with another human being if that person would be shamed by being seen with you, such as when one chases after one's friend in order to give him or her *tzedakah*, for that friend would be embarrassed if another saw that he or she needed [charity].[4]

To shame another person in public, even when such an act is based on good intentions, is a terrible sin. As we read, Yechiel thinks it is akin to the spilling of blood. If one has a friend in financial or in any other type of trouble, it is far better to help him or her privately, removed from public view, so as to avoid any unnecessary embarrassment to that person.

BOSHET IN JEWISH MYSTICISM

The concept of *boshet* figures significantly in the worldview of Rabbi Dov Baer, the Maggid of Mezhirech. As a Jewish mystic, the Maggid was steeped in the teachings of classical Kabbalah, but as a man living near the end of the eighteenth century, he was also profoundly interested in the *psychological* application of these teachings.

The notion of shame as a spiritual virtue appears frequently in the Maggid's writings. Take, for instance, his interpretation of a verse from Psalms, "The beginning of wisdom is the fear of God." (111:10) The Maggid writes:

It is known that wisdom is [the letter] *yod*, the smallest of all the letters, since it shrinks and contracts itself because it is the first of them all and close to the Cause of all causes…. Because it is [thus] close to God, out of great fear and shame it contracts and restricts itself.[5]

The Maggid here associates the letter *yod*, the smallest letter in the Hebrew alphabet, with the kabbalistic *sefirah*—"divine emanation"—of wisdom. As the second to highest level of divine manifestation (the highest is called *keter*—"crown"), the *sefirah* of wisdom rests just below the Godhead, the "Cause of all causes." In such close proximity to the divine mystery, the letter *yod*, wisdom, has no choice but to bow down before it in fear and shame.

Just as Yechiel connects the virtue of *boshet* with the idea of fear, so, too, does the Maggid. It is shame and fear that serve as the psychological catalysts for the act of "contraction," or humility before another. For Yechiel, shame/fear saves one from sin; for the Maggid, it marks true wisdom—the proof that one has reached the highest of spiritual levels.

The association of shame with wisdom has important consequences. On the human level, it means that a mature relationship is possible only if one person is able to "make room" for another. Each of us must give the other the space to live and grow. On the divine level, it means that spiritual wisdom does not result from the knowledge of God but rather from the absence of that knowledge. In other words, when we stand in the presence of the Mystery we call God, shame is our most appropriate response. It is the recognition of the partition between our limitations and God's limitlessness that indicates we have achieved true enlightenment.

Boshet: A Case Study

As we have seen, the virtue of *boshet* can be viewed in both a positive and negative way. Unlike many of the other spiritual virtues, the value of *boshet* depends heavily on the context in which it is experienced. Let us first take a look at *boshet* as a positive attribute.

MEETING WITH THE BOSS

Joseph K. is the newest employee of an advertising firm. After only two weeks on the job, he has been called in by one of the company's executives. Although having a meeting with one of the superiors is fairly standard practice at the firm, Joseph senses that he has done something wrong. He is nervous but decides to be strong and stand up for himself, no matter what happens at the meeting.

After some preliminary small talk, Joseph's supervisor informs him that he has made some mistakes on his current project. The executive tells Joseph that his mistakes are the result of inexperience and that he needs to be made aware of them so as to prevent his making similar errors in the future. The supervisor then offers Joseph some constructive advice on how to do the project better. Although Joseph's job is not threatened, his ego is. He feels that he is a talented employee and that he could easily fill his supervisor's role at the firm if he had a little more experience. Joseph's supervisor asks him if he has anything to say.

———— *HOW SHOULD JOSEPH RESPOND?* ————

QUESTIONS FOR DISCUSSION

1. What exactly is at stake for Joseph in this situation? What could he gain and what could he lose by defending his efforts and rejecting his supervisor's advice?

2. Should Joseph defend his actions? Would it be better for him professionally to "save face" or accept the criticism? What about spiritually?

3. How might Joseph demonstrate the virtue of *boshet* in this situation?

4. How might *boshet* help him in this context?

5. If shame can save a person from sin, which sin might it save Joseph from in this situation?

6. How can shame help one grow professionally? Spiritually?

7. Could the discomfort one feels while experiencing shame be beneficial? How?

Boshet: A Case Study

Let us now examine *boshet* in one of its negative manifestations.

THE DINNER PARTY

The Religion Department of Rogue State University is holding its annual holiday dinner party at a local restaurant. Karl is a tenured professor on the faculty, and Pozzo, a young, outspoken member of the department, is one of his new colleagues. Earlier in the week, Pozzo had made several derogatory remarks about Karl's academic views and about the "old school," of which Karl is a senior spokesperson. Pozzo's remarks seemed to be a deliberate insult. Karl finds Pozzo pompous and offensive, with few redeeming qualities.

At the dinner party, Karl overhears Pozzo make a remark on a subject that Pozzo knows little about and on which Karl is an expert. Karl has the perfect opportunity to interrupt Pozzo's conversation and make him look like a fool. Karl tells himself that Pozzo deserves to be put down because he has shown no remorse over his past remarks. But if Karl were to correct Pozzo in public, the new faculty member would be utterly humiliated in front of his friends, family, and colleagues.

———— WHAT SHOULD KARL DO? ————

QUESTIONS FOR DISCUSSION

1. What factors should Karl consider before he acts?

2. Is it better to absorb a wrong or to seek vengeance?

3. How is shaming a person with intent different from accidentally shaming someone?

4. By shaming Pozzo, how would Karl help/harm him?

5. By shaming Pozzo, would Karl also bring shame upon himself? If so, how?

6. Are there other means to remedy a wrong? What are they? Why might they be better than shaming someone?

---

[1] *Otzar Sefer Chasidim, Boshet*
[2] Ibid.
[3] Ibid
[4] Ibid.
[5] *Likutim Yekarim*, pp. 105b-106a

41

Emunah

אֱמוּנָה

Come, my students, and I will instruct you in the virtue of faith. Know, my students, that the virtue of faith [emunah] is honored and very great in the eyes of God. For everyone who deals with others honestly merits and sits in the section of the Holy One. As it is written: "My eyes are on the trusty men of the land, to have them sit with Me. He who walks on the way of the blameless shall be in My service." [Psalms 101:6] And not only that, but the Holy One always looks upon the honest ones [ba'alei emunah]. As it is written: "O God, Your eyes look for integrity." [Jeremiah 5:3] And God is associated with this virtue. As it is written: "A faithful God, never false." [Deuteronomy 32:4]

בָּנַי, בֹּאוּ וַאֲלַמֶּדְכֶם מַעֲלַת הָאֱמוּנָה. דְּעוּ בָּנַי, כִּי מַעֲלַת הָאֱמוּנָה מַעֲלָה נִכְבֶּדֶת וּגְדוֹלָה מְאֹד בְּעֵינֵי הַמָּקוֹם. שֶׁכָּל הַנּוֹשֵׂא וְנוֹתֵן עִם הַבְּרִיּוֹת בֶּאֱמוּנָה, זוֹכֶה וְיוֹשֵׁב בִּמְחִיצָתוֹ שֶׁל הַקָּדוֹשׁ־בָּרוּךְ־הוּא, כָּעִנְיָן שֶׁנֶּאֱמַר, עֵינַי בְּנֶאֶמְנֵי־אֶרֶץ לָשֶׁבֶת עִמָּדִי הֹלֵךְ בְּדֶרֶךְ תָּמִים הוּא יְשָׁרְתֵנִי. וְלֹא עוֹד אֶלָּא שֶׁהַקָּדוֹשׁ־בָּרוּךְ־הוּא נוֹתֵן עֵינָיו תָּמִיד בְּבַעֲלֵי־אֱמוּנָה, כָּעִנְיָן שֶׁנֶּאֱמַר, יְיָ עֵינֶיךָ הֲלוֹא לֶאֱמוּנָה. וּבְמַעֲלַת הַמִּדָּה הַזֹּאת, נִתְיַחֵס בָּהּ הַמָּקוֹם, כָּעִנְיָן שֶׁנֶּאֱמַר, אֵל אֱמוּנָה וְאֵין עָוֶל וְגוֹ'.

My students, come and see how great is the power of loyalty/fidelity, for even the ministering angels do not merit to stand in a place where those of strong faith are found. Therefore, the sages, of blessed memory, say in an aggadah: "There is no sitting in the heavens." [Genesis Rabbah 65:7] As it is written: "And their [the heavenly creatures'] legs were fused into one single rigid leg" [Ezekiel 1:7] that could not bend. "I approached one of the attendants [ka'amaya]—those who stand [kayemaya]." [Daniel 7:16] "Seraphim stood in attendance on God." [Isaiah 6:2] "With all the hosts of

בָּנַי, בֹּאוּ וּרְאוּ כַּמָּה גָדוֹל כֹּחַ הַנֶּאֱמָנוּת, שֶׁבַּמָּקוֹם שֶׁבַּעֲלֵי אֲמָנָה עוֹמְדִין, אֲפִילוּ מַלְאֲכֵי־הַשָּׁרֵת אֵין זוֹכִין לָהּ. שֶׁכָּךְ אָמְרוּ חֲכָמֵינוּ זִכְרוֹנָם לִבְרָכָה בָּאַגָּדָה, אֵין יְשִׁיבָה לְמַעְלָה, שֶׁנֶּאֱמַר, וְרַגְלֵיהֶם רֶגֶל יְשָׁרָה, אֵין לָהֶן קְפִיצִין. קָרְבֵת עַל־חַד מִן קָאֲמַיָּא־קָיְמַיָּא. שְׂרָפִים עֹמְדִים מִמַּעַל לוֹ. וְכָל־צְבָא הַשָּׁמַיִם עֹמְדִים עָלָיו. וְנָתַתִּי לְךָ מַהְלְכִים בֵּין הָעֹמְדִים הָאֵלֶּה. וְאִלּוּ בְּבַעֲלֵי־אֲמָנָה כְּתִיב, לָשֶׁבֶת עִמָּדִי.

heaven standing to the right and left of God." [I Kings 22:19] "And I will give you the ability to walk among these [angels] who stand." [Zechariah 3:7] However, concerning the ones [humans] who are strong in faith, the verse states: "My eyes are on the trusty men of the land, that they may *sit* at my side." [Psalms 101:6]

And what is faith? The beginning of *emunah* occurs when a person will trust [be secure] in God and will not fear anything and will be satisfied with the divine decree and will give himself and his spirit to God, so that all of his [business] dealings and his words will be faithful and upright, and what is true he will admit, and what is false he will deny, and he will not rush to get rich; rather he trusts in God in all his matters. As it is written: "Trust in God and do good; abide in the land and remain loyal." [Psalms 37:2] And what he promises he should fulfill to the best of his ability.

Justice [truth, right] results from this praiseworthy virtue [of honesty]. For all of a person's weights and his measures should be true. As it is written: "You shall have honest balances, honest weights, an honest *ephah*, and an honest *hin*." [Leviticus 19:36] And all his words and all his matters should be prepared and arranged according to what is right, and he should not request any degree or increase over others. And I will say that the fruit of honesty is wealth. And [according to the Midrash on Psalms 7:11], the fruit of deceit is poverty and destitution.

וּמַה הִיא הָאֱמוּנָה? תְּחִלַּת הָאֱמוּנָה, שֶׁיִּבְטַח הָאָדָם בֵּאלֹהִים, וְלֹא יִירָא מִשּׁוּם דָּבָר, וְיִרְצֶה בִּגְזֵרַת הַמָּקוֹם, וְיִמְסֹר עַצְמוֹ וְנַפְשׁוֹ אֵלָיו, וְשֶׁיִּהְיֶה מַשָּׂאוֹ וּמַתָּנוֹ וּדְבָרָיו כֻּלָּם בֶּאֱמוּנָה וּבְיֹשֶׁר, וְיֹאמַר עַל הֵן הֵן וְעַל לָאו לָאו, וְאֵינוֹ אָץ לְהַעֲשִׁיר, אֶלָּא שֶׁבִּטְחוֹנוֹ בְּהַקָּדוֹשׁ־בָּרוּךְ־הוּא בְּכָל עִנְיָנָיו, כָּעִנְיָן שֶׁנֶּאֱמַר, בְּטַח בַּייָ וַעֲשֵׂה־טוֹב שְׁכָן־אֶרֶץ וּרְעֵה אֱמוּנָה. וּמַה שֶּׁיַּבְטִיחַ, יָקַיֵּם בִּיכָלְתּוֹ.

וּמִסְּעִיפֵי הַמִּדָּה הַמְשֻׁבַּחַת הַזֹּאת, יוֹצֵא הַצֶּדֶק, שֶׁיִּהְיוּ כָּל מִשְׁקְלוֹתָיו שֶׁל אָדָם וְכָל מִדּוֹתָיו, צֶדֶק, כָּעִנְיָן שֶׁנֶּאֱמַר, מֹאזְנֵי צֶדֶק אַבְנֵי־צֶדֶק אֵיפַת צֶדֶק וְהִין צֶדֶק יִהְיֶה לָכֶם. וְכָל דְּבָרָיו וְעִנְיָנָיו, מְתֻקָּנִים וּמְסֻדָּרִים עַל פִּי הַצֶּדֶק, וְאֵינוֹ מְבַקֵּשׁ שׁוּם מַעֲלָה וְיִתְרוֹן עַל בְּנֵי־אָדָם. וְאוֹמַר, כִּי פְּרִי הַנֶּאֱמָנוּת, הָעֹשֶׁר. וּפְרִי הַכַּחַשׁ, הָרֵישׁ וְהָעֹנִי.

43

And a person must conduct himself with faithfulness and righteousness even in mundane matters that he conducts with his colleague [*chavero*]. Thus said our sages, of blessed memory: "What does the Torah want to teach us when it says in Leviticus 19:36, 'an honest *ephah* and an honest *hin*'? Isn't *hin* included in *ephah*? Rather, it is to teach us that your yes should be true and your no should be true." [*Baba Metzia* 49a] And, furthermore, the sages, of blessed memory, said: "Anyone who conducts his business with words [i.e., one whose word is his bond] should not give his word to one who habitually breaks his word." [*Yerushalmi Baba Metzia* 90b, 12b] However, the sages said: "When anyone abandons [wastes] his words, the spirit of wisdom moves [away] from him." [*Tosefta Baba Metzia*, chapter 3]

וְצָרִיךְ לוֹ לָאָדָם לִנְהוֹג עַצְמוֹ בֶּאֱמוּנָה וּבְצֶדֶק אֲפִילוּ בִּדְבָרִים בְּעָלְמָא שֶׁנּוֹהֵג עִם חֲבֵרוֹ. שֶׁכָּךְ אָמְרוּ חֲכָמֵינוּ זִכְרוֹנָם לִבְרָכָה, מַה תַּלְמוּד לוֹמַר, אֵיפַת צֶדֶק וְהִין צֶדֶק יִהְיֶה לָכֶם, וַהֲלֹא הִין בִּכְלָל אֵיפָה הִיא? אֶלָּא, שֶׁיְּהֵא הֵן שֶׁלְּךָ צֶדֶק וְלָאו שֶׁלְּךָ צֶדֶק. וְעוֹד אָמְרוּ חֲכָמֵינוּ זִכְרוֹנָם לִבְרָכָה, כָּל הַנּוֹשֵׂא וְנוֹתֵן בִּדְבָרִים, אֵין מוֹסְרִין אוֹתוֹ לְמִי־שֶׁפָּרַע. אֲבָל אָמְרוּ חֲכָמִים, כָּל הַמְבַטֵּל אֶת דְּבָרָיו, אֵין רוּחַ חֲכָמִים נוֹחָה הֵימֶנּוּ.

And know, my students, that from *emunah* endurance is born, that one suffers/endures with love everything that the Holy One will decree upon him, both good and bad, and endures what the Holy One forbids him and believes that God will pay him his reward in the future. As one sage said: "Suffering/endurance is of two types: the suffering of troubles and the suffering of what the Creator has forbidden you." [*Mivchar Hapeninim* 9:3] And he said: "Memory is of two types: the memory of the suffering at the moment of the wound and, even greater than that, the memory of the restrictions that God has placed upon you."

וּדְעוּ לָכֶם בָּנַי, כִּי מִן הָאֱמוּנָה, תִּוָּלֵד הַסֵּבֶל, שֶׁסּוֹבֵל מֵאַהֲבָה כָּל מַה שֶּׁיִּגְזוֹר הַבּוֹרֵא עָלָיו הֵן טוֹב הֵן רַע, וְסוֹבֵל בְּעַצְמוֹ מִכָּל מַה שֶּׁאָסַר הַבּוֹרֵא עָלָיו, וּמַאֲמִין בּוֹ שֶׁיְּשַׁלֵּם לוֹ שְׂכָרוֹ לְעָתִיד לָבוֹא. כְּמוֹ שֶׁאָמַר חָכָם אֶחָד, הַסֵּבֶל שְׁנֵי מִינִין, סֵבֶל הַצָּרוֹת, וְהַסֵּבֶל בְּמַה שֶּׁאָסַר הַבּוֹרֵא עָלֶיךָ. וְאָמַר, הַזִּכָּרוֹן, שְׁנֵי מִינִין. זִכְרוֹן הַסֵּבֶל בְּעֵת הַפֶּגַע, וְטוֹב מִמֶּנּוּ זִכְרוֹן הַבּוֹרֵא בְּמַה שֶּׁאָסַר עָלֶיךָ לִהְיוֹת מַבְדִּיל בֵּינְךָ לְבֵינוֹ.

Happy are the faithful ones who bring merit to themselves and the whole world through their faith. As it is written: "Roam the streets of Jerusalem, search the squares, look about and take note. If you will find a man, if there is anyone who acts justly and seeks integrity [*emunah*], I will pardon her." [Jeremiah 5:1] And not only that, but the faithful one also merits life in this world and in the World to Come. As it is written: "If he has followed My laws and kept My rules to act honestly, he is righteous. Such a man shall live [*chayo yichyeh*], declares God." [Ezekiel 18:9] He will live [*chayo*] in this world; he will live [*yichyeh*] in the World to Come.

אַשְׁרֵיהֶן בַּעֲלֵי אֱמוּנָה, שֶׁזּוֹכִין לָהֶן וּלְכָל הָעוֹלָם כֻּלּוֹ בֶּאֱמוּנָתָן, כָּעִנְיָן שֶׁנֶּאֱמַר, שׁוֹטְטוּ בְּחוּצוֹת יְרוּשָׁלַיִם וּרְאוּ־נָא וּדְעוּ וּבַקְּשׁוּ בִּרְחוֹבוֹתֶיהָ אִם־תִּמְצְאוּ אִישׁ אִם־יֵשׁ עֹשֶׂה מִשְׁפָּט מְבַקֵּשׁ אֱמוּנָה וְאֶסְלַח לָהּ. וְלֹא עוֹד אֶלָּא, שֶׁזּוֹכֶה לְחַיִּים בָּעוֹלָם־הַזֶּה וְלָעוֹלָם־הַבָּא, שֶׁנֶּאֱמַר, בְּחֻקּוֹתַי הָלַךְ וּמִשְׁפָּטַי שָׁמַר לַעֲשׂוֹת אֱמֶת צַדִּיק הוּא חָיֹה יִחְיֶה נְאֻם אֲדֹנָי אֱלֹהִים. חָיֹה בָּעוֹלָם־הַזֶּה, יִחְיֶה לָעוֹלָם־הַבָּא.

Therefore, my students, be careful with this virtue, so that you will inherit this world and the World to Come. And God will enable us to succeed in this virtue because of God's great mercy.

[The opposite of *emunah* is *gneivah* (larceny, theft) and *gazlanut* (robbery).]

לָכֵן בָּנַי, הֱווּ זְהִירִין בְּמַעֲלַת הַמִּדָּה הַזֹּאת, כְּדֵי שֶׁתִּירְשׁוּ חַיֵּי הָעוֹלָם־הַזֶּה וְתִנְחֲלוּ חַיֵּי הָעוֹלָם־הַבָּא. וְהָאֱלֹהִים יַצְלִיחֵנוּ בָהּ בְּרַחֲמָיו הָרַבִּים.

Commentary

Anyone who has ever thought seriously about religion knows, or at least intuits, that *emunah*—"faith"—is its foundation. A religion that does not consider faith to be one of its key virtues would seem to be an empty vessel. Yet the association of faith with belief, as we have come to understand it today, differs in several ways from the classical Jewish definition of faith, which connects that virtue far more to interpersonal notions like trust and reliance.

Yechiel first describes *emunah* on the human level in terms of honesty. Whoever deals with other people honestly, whoever interacts with them with *faith*fulness, merits a seat next to God in the divine court. From this we see that *emunah* is not understood simply as a spiritual "possession" (e.g., *x* has faith in *y*) but rather as an attitude toward interpersonal relationships that must be acted out in real time and in real life. The *ba'alei emunah*—the "honest ones"—serve as the mirror image of the Divine Personality, who is referred to as *El emunah*—"a faithful God."

The above passage relates to the role *emunah* plays in human affairs. But what role does *emunah* play in the relationship between human beings and God? Yechiel writes that *emunah* begins when a person trusts/relies upon God. As a result of this sense of security, that person is able to overcome all personal anxieties and fears. This idea is reminiscent of the final phrase in the hymn *Adon Olam*, in which we recite the words "*Adonai* is with me, and I shall not fear."

Emunah also yields other benefits. The feeling of security that allows a person to transcend his or her fears also gives that person the strength and courage to "be satisfied with the divine decree," with his or her lot in life. Being able to accept one's existential situation—with all of its problems, limitations, and pains—is difficult for all of us. Trust in God, however (and not just the belief that there is a God), enables a Jew to "give himself and his spirit to God." Through submission/surrender to God's care and God's judgment, a Jew liberates himself or herself from dissatisfaction, dishonesty, and worldly desires.

The virtue of *emunah* also leads to other religious virtues, such as justice, *tzedek*. The Jew who acts with faithfulness will say what he or she means to say and do what he or she promises to do: A yes will mean yes and a no will mean no, and all of his or her weights and measures will be accurate and true. In short, he or she will be trustworthy and strive to do what is right, what is fair, and what is just. He or she will not want or ask for any special treatment or privilege that others do not have. The saying that "virtue is its own reward" would certainly apply to the *ba'al emunah*, who views honesty and trustworthiness as treasures and the world's only true wealth.

Although the *ba'al emunah* must act with faithfulness and truth even with regard to the most mundane of matters, there are some situations in which he or she is not obligated to give his or her word, even though the word of a *ba'al emunah* is "as good as gold." One of these situations involves dealing with someone who is dishonest and habitually breaks his or her word. However, the sages argue that one must be truthful at *all* times, for when a person "abandons" his or her words, when he or she forsakes honesty, the "spirit of wisdom" leaves the soul. If, as the Kabbalists claim, words themselves contain sparks of divinity, then to misuse them is to abuse the sanctity of their Creator.

Another quality that results from *emunah* is patience or endurance. A person who has reached this level will have gained the ability to endure with love everything—both good and bad—that God has decreed for him or her. *Emunah* will also give that person the strength and discipline to refrain from those things that God has forbidden, knowing that his or her behavior will be rewarded by God in the future. Yechiel notes that there are thus two types of long-suffering: that which involves enduring pain and that which involves resisting forbidden desires.

The faithful ones, the *ba'alei emunah*, will do more than just bring merit onto themselves. Through their very faithfulness, they will also bring merit to the whole world. The spiritual power of a single faithful Jew is great enough to encompass the rest of humanity. And more than that, the *ba'al emunah* will, through the acceptance of his or her situation in life, merit eternal life in the World to Come. The virtue of *emunah*, therefore, has both universal and particular benefits: It helps redeem the world and it leads to the salvation of the soul.

EMUNAH IN JEWISH PIETISM

The importance of *emunah* to one's ability to lead a life of Jewish piety was a key tenet of the Chasidei Ashkenaz, the pietists of medieval Germany. It was not until the Middle Ages, when the challenge of philosophical atheism arose, that Jewish thinkers, in their defense of theism, began to discuss the notion of *emunah* in terms of belief in a God rather than faithfulness (which already assumes God's existence). Judah the Pious, one of the movement's greatest leaders, writes:

> A righteous person should never think of himself as poor. If a man [believes] that his wife has become pregnant by him, and [laments], "Where will I find the means [to support the child]?" this is the result of his lack of faith, for the Holy One, blessed be He, provides a woman with milk for her baby once it leaves its mother's womb. Thus it is written in the *Mechilta* [a collection of *midrashim* on the Book of Exodus], "Whoever has food to eat today and asks, 'What will I eat tomorrow?' this results from lack of faith."[1]

In the above context, *emunah* refers not so much to a person's fidelity to a relationship (faithfulness) as to one's belief (faith) in a God who will provide for all of life's needs. The *tzadik*, the person who is truly righteous, should never consider himself or herself poor. Whether he or she is required to assume a new financial burden as a result of the birth of an unexpected child or some other unexpected event, as a righteous Jew he or she should not despair. Instead, he or she should have faith that there is a God and that God will ultimately take care of things. Because the *ba'al emunah* believes this, faith enables him or her to live in the present and be satisfied with his or her existential situation.

Although the above passage is about faith in God's reality, the following text shows that the Chasidei Ashkenaz were also concerned with the role of *emunah* in interpersonal relations.

> There is the story of a man who would never study Torah except on Shabbat because on all the weekdays he would conduct business. He questioned a sage, "What [virtue] is it that will outweigh [all my time spent in business matters] and bring me eternal life in the World to Come?" The sage answered him, "You who engage in business…must act toward all others with *emunah*."[2]

Redemption is possible via every sphere of human activity. Even the person who devotes nearly all of his or her waking hours to business matters and virtually ignores the religious obligations like study and prayer can find divine reward for his or her actions. It is not *what* we do in life but rather *how* we do it that is most significant to God. If one's life is defined by the conduct of business transactions, then what matters most is that one makes those transactions fairly and honestly with *emunah*. Only then is redemption possible. And therein lies one of Jewish spirituality's core messages—the idea that even the most ordinary of things can be sanctified.

EMUNAH IN JEWISH MYSTICISM

For Rabbi Zaddok ha-Kohen, *emunah* is a spiritual virtue that holds the power not only to redeem the soul in the hereafter but also to free our minds in the present. A Jewish thinker who lived near the turn of the twentieth century, Zaddok was exposed to a concept of *emunah* that had long been discussed in terms of belief rather than as mere reliance on a God whose existence was taken for granted. His writings thus reflect a much more modern approach to the topic of faith. Zaddok writes:

> *Emunah* is a great foundation by which to save a man from empty fantasies and idle talk, especially during the study of Torah and the time of prayer.[3]

It is clear from this text that Zaddok views *emunah* as a spiritual attribute with dimensions that touch the most basic of Jewish activities—study and prayer. Faith, when "exercised," has a practical side. While a Jew is focused firmly on God, his or her ability to "drown out" distractions, whether psychological or interpersonal in nature, becomes easy. The *ba'al emunah* thus maximizes his or her divine merit in two important ways: first, through the belief in God that is itself a religious commandment and second, through the performance of the Jewish obligations of study and prayer, which *emunah* can only intensify.

Zaddok continues to explore the psychological benefits of *emunah*:

> Just as a man needs to have faith in God, may He be blessed, so, too, must he afterward have faith in himself. This means that God, may

He be blessed, has business with him—that he not become an idle worker.... A person needs to have faith [in himself] because his soul comes from the Source of Life, and God, may He be blessed, takes pleasure from...it [his soul] when it performs His will.[4]

From the time of the revelation at Mount Sinai, the people of Israel and God have entered into a contract, or "covenant," with each other. According to the Torah, if the Jewish people follow God's will and observe God's commandments, God will ultimately redeem them. For many Jews, this has been a daunting task. Rather than trying our best, too many of us have simply given up hope of even coming close to fulfilling our part of the covenant. But faith in God can give us faith in ourselves and the strength to labor on without feeling hopeless and becoming sluggish. Since all our souls have their source in God, a spark of divinity resides within each of us. It is *emunah* that holds the power to kindle this ever-present spark into a fire strong enough to inspire us onward.

Emunah: A Case Study

If there ever was an Age of Faith, it is surely not the one in which we are living. All over the world and especially in the West, it seems that belief in and reliance upon God have never been weaker (except within the growing but still relatively small fundamentalist movements). Materialism, secularism, and convenience appear to be the idols of modernity. Those people who possess or strive for *emunah* are rare birds indeed and are sometimes the objects of ridicule and scorn.

BLIND FAITH?

Rick is a middle-aged worker at an automobile plant who has just received notice that his position has been terminated as a result of downsizing. He has worked at the plant for nearly two decades, never making any trouble for management because he felt they paid him fair wages. Six months ago his wife left him, and she now has custody of their two children. He lives alone and wonders what skills he has to offer other employers.

Despite his situation, Rick retains a strong faith in God. He believes, as he always has, that God exists and that God will take care of him regardless of how tough times become. When his luck had been down in the past, he managed to make it through and move on with his life, believing that in the end everything would turn out all right and that good actions would be rewarded. His friends make fun of him, calling him naive and passive. They think that he is too weak to stand up and "fight for his rights" and that he accepts his lot too readily.

———— *IS RICK MAKING A MISTAKE?* ————

QUESTIONS FOR DISCUSSION

1. Do you consider Rick's faith in God to be the result of psychological weakness or spiritual strength?

2. Do you think that you would have Rick's faith in the face of his current troubles? Do you think that Rick's faith is unrealistic?

3. One of the criticisms of having "blind faith" is that it can lead a person to passivity and inaction even when that person is confronted with injustice (like low wages). Do you think that this criticism is valid? Are there are other forms of faith that avoid this issue?

4. Without faith, how might Rick react to his setbacks? What, if any, are the consequences of spiritual doubt to our lives?

5. If Rick's faith is not rewarded (i.e., if there is no God to repay good actions), can we say that Rick has lived foolishly? Has he lost anything by having his faith? What, if anything, might he have gained?

6. Do you think it is possible to survive life's hardships without some kind of faith? In what or whom other than God might a person have faith? Why might having faith in those things seem more acceptable than having faith in God?

---

[1] *Otzar Sefer Chasidim, Emunah*

[2] Ibid.

[3] *Kitvei Rabbi Zaddok ha-Kohen, Emunah*

[4] Ibid.

Temimut

תְּמִימוּת

My students, come and I will teach you about the virtue of integrity. Know, my students, that the virtue of integrity [*temimut*] is great and dear. For everyone who conducts himself with integrity, God chooses his service. As it is written: "He who follows the way of the blameless shall be in My service." [Psalms 101:6] Thus Moses, our teacher, may he rest in peace, commanded on the matter of integrity/blamelessness. As it is written: "You must be wholehearted [*tamim*] before your God." [Deuteronomy 18:13]

בָּנֵי, בֹּאוּ וַאֲלַמֶּדְכֶם מַעֲלַת הַתְּמִימוּת. דְּעוּ בָּנֵי, כִּי מַעֲלַת הַתְּמִימוּת, מַעֲלָה גְּדוֹלָה וִיקָרָה. שֶׁכָּל מִי שֶׁהוֹלֵךְ בִּתְמִימוּת, הַקָּדוֹשׁ־בָּרוּךְ־הוּא בּוֹחֵר בְּשֵׁרוּתוֹ, כָּעִנְיָן שֶׁנֶּאֱמַר, הֹלֵךְ בְּדֶרֶךְ תָּמִים הוּא יְשָׁרְתֵנִי. וְכֵן צִוָּה מֹשֶׁה רַבֵּנוּ עָלָיו הַשָּׁלוֹם עַל עֵסֶק הַתְּמִימוּת, כָּעִנְיָן שֶׁנֶּאֱמַר, תָּמִים תִּהְיֶה עִם יְיָ אֱלֹהֶיךָ.

And what is *temimut*? That a person should speak words without deceitfulness and his business dealings should be without deceit and fraud, and his mouth and his heart are equal. Anyone who is one way in his mouth and another in his heart cannot be called *tam*. Rather, such a person can be called a hypocrite/flatterer and a swindler/scoundrel without a doubt. As it is written: "Deceit is in the mind/heart of those who plan evil." [Proverbs 12:20]

וּמַה הוּא הַתְּמִימוּת? שֶׁיְדַבֵּר הָאָדָם דְּבָרָיו בְּלִי רַמָּאוּת, וּמַשָּׂאוֹ וּמַתָּנוֹ בְּלִי רַמָּאוּת וּמִרְמָה, וּפִיו וְלִבּוֹ שָׁוִין. שֶׁכָּל מִי שֶׁהוּא אֶחָד בַּפֶּה וְאֶחָד בַּלֵּב, אֵינוֹ נִקְרָא תָם, אֶלָּא שֶׁנִּקְרָא חָנֵף וְרַמַּאי בְּלִי סָפֵק, כָּעִנְיָן שֶׁנֶּאֱמַר, מִרְמָה בְּלֶב־חֹרְשֵׁי־רָע וְגוֹ'.

Great is the virtue of *temimut* before God. For God wants and delights in everyone who conducts himself with *temimut*. As it is written: "Those whose way is blameless please

גְּדוֹלָה הִיא מִדַּת הַתְּמִימוּת לִפְנֵי הַמָּקוֹם. שֶׁכָּל מִי שֶׁהוֹלֵךְ בִּתְמִימוּת, הַקָּדוֹשׁ־בָּרוּךְ־הוּא רוֹצֶה וְחָפֵץ בּוֹ, כָּעִנְיָן

God." [Proverbs 11:20] And not only that, but because of integrity, a person straightens out his ways. As it is written: "The righteousness of the blameless man makes straight his way." [Proverbs 11:5] And God guards from sin and iniquity anyone who conducts himself with integrity [*temimut*] with God and with others, and he [that person] dwells in calm and security like wine as it ages. As it is written: "I have been blameless toward God and have guarded myself from sinning." [Psalms 18:24] And it is also written: "And You support me because of my integrity and let me abide in Your presence forever." [Psalms 41:13]

And from this praiseworthy virtue emerges the virtue of truth [*emet*], which is among the thirteen attributes ascribed to the Creator. As it is written: "Long-suffering, abundant in mercy and truth." [Exodus 34:6] And moreover, truth is God's seal/signature, for you find that *alef* is the first of the letters in the Hebrew alphabet, *mem* is in the middle, and *tav* is at the end.

[The author now concerns himself with the opposite of *temimut*, which is *rama'ut*— deceitfulness or acts of deceitfulness, fraudulence, and hypocrisy.]

Come and see how difficult this characteristic of dishonesty/falsehood can be. For because of the slander and lies that the spies brought out about *Eretz Yisrael*, the decree that every Israelite from the age of twenty and older would perish in the wilderness was sealed.

שֶׁנֶּאֱמַר, וּרְצוֹנוֹ תְּמִימֵי דָרֶךְ. וְלֹא עוֹד אֶלָּא, שֶׁבִּשְׁבִיל הַתְּמִימוּת, מְיַשֵׁר הָאָדָם אֶת דְּרָכָיו, שֶׁנֶּאֱמַר, צִדְקַת תָּמִים תְּיַשֵׁר דַּרְכּוֹ וְגוֹ'. וְכָל מִי שֶׁהוֹלֵךְ בִּתְמִימוּת עִם הָאֵל וְהַבְּרִיּוֹת, הַקָּדוֹשׁ-בָּרוּךְ-הוּא מְשַׁמְּרוֹ מִן הַחֲטָאִים וְהָעֲוֹנוֹת, וְיוֹשֵׁב שָׁקֵט וּבוֹטֵחַ כַּיַּיִן שׁוֹקֵט עַל שְׁמָרָיו, כָּעִנְיָן שֶׁנֶּאֱמַר, וָאֱהִי תָמִים עִמּוֹ וָאֶשְׁתַּמֵּר מֵעֲוֹנִי. וְכֵן הוּא אוֹמֵר, וַאֲנִי בְּתֻמִּי תָּמַכְתָּ בִּי וַתַּצִּיבֵנִי לְפָנֶיךָ לְעוֹלָם.

וּמִן הַמִּדָּה הַמְשֻׁבַּחַת הַזֹּאת, יוֹצֵאת מִדַּת הָאֱמֶת שֶׁהִיא מִשְּׁלֹשׁ-עֶשְׂרֵה מִדּוֹת שֶׁנִּתְיַחֵס בָּהֶן הַבּוֹרֵא, כָּעִנְיָן שֶׁנֶּאֱמַר, אֶרֶךְ אַפַּיִם וְרַב-חֶסֶד וֶאֱמֶת. וְלֹא עוֹד אֶלָּא שֶׁחוֹתָמוֹ שֶׁל הַקָּדוֹשׁ-בָּרוּךְ-הוּא אֱמֶת, שֶׁכֵּן אַתָּה מוֹצֵא אָלֶ"ף בְּרֹאשׁ הָאוֹתִיּוֹת, מֵ"ם בָּאֶמְצָעָן, תָּי"ו בְּסוֹפָן.

צְאוּ וּרְאוּ כַּמָּה קָשָׁה מִדַּת הַשֶּׁקֶר, שֶׁבִּשְׁבִיל הַדִּבָּה וְהַשֶּׁקֶר שֶׁהוֹצִיאוּ הַמְרַגְּלִים עַל אֶרֶץ-יִשְׂרָאֵל, נִתְחַתֵּם גְּזַר-דִּינָן שֶׁל יִשְׂרָאֵל לָמוּת בַּמִּדְבָּר מִבֶּן עֶשְׂרִים שָׁנָה וָמָעְלָה.

Dishonesty/falsehood is a hated behavior before God, for anyone who runs after falsehood will not receive the presence of God. As the sages, of blessed memory, said: "Four groups will not receive the presence of God. They are the mockers, the liars, the hypocrites/flatterers, and the gossipers." [*Sotah* 42a]

מִדָּה שְׂנוּאָה הִיא הַשֶּׁקֶר לִפְנֵי הַמָּקוֹם, שֶׁכָּל מִי שֶׁהוּא לָהוּט אַחַר הַשֶּׁקֶר, אֵינוֹ מְקַבֵּל פְּנֵי שְׁכִינָה, שֶׁכָּךְ אָמְרוּ חֲכָמֵינוּ זִכְרוֹנָם לִבְרָכָה, אַרְבַּע כִּתּוֹת אֵינָן מְקַבְּלוֹת פְּנֵי שְׁכִינָה. וְאֵלּוּ הֵן, כַּת לֵצִים, כַּת שַׁקָּרִים, כַּת חֲנֵפִים, כַּת מְסַפְּרֵי לָשׁוֹן־הָרָע.

And one pious man said to his disciples: "If you were not guilty of some iniquity, I would fear something greater/worse even than iniquity." They asked him: "And what is that?" He answered them: "Arrogance and flattery."

וְאָמַר חָסִיד אֶחָד לְתַלְמִידָיו, אִלּוּ לֹא הָיָה לָכֶם עָוֹן, הָיִיתִי מְפַחֵד עֲלֵיכֶם בְּדָבָר שֶׁהוּא גָדוֹל מִן הֶעָוֹן. אָמְרוּ לוֹ, וּמַה הוּא? אָמַר לָהֶם, הַגַּאֲוָת וְהַחֹנֶף.

And despite the fact that God and humanity greatly despise hypocrisy, in spite of that, a person is permitted to be hypocrit- ical to [flatter] evil people because of the fear or because of the terror one fears or feels of them.... Thus Jacob, our ancestor, may he rest in peace, flattered Esau when he said to him, "Seeing your face is like seeing the face of God, and you were pleased with me." [Genesis 33:10]

וְאַף־עַל־פִּי שֶׁמִּדַּת הַחֲנֵפָה דָּבָר שָׂנאוּי מְאֹד בְּעֵינֵי הַמָּקוֹם וּבְעֵינֵי הַבְּרִיּוֹת, אַף־ עַל־פִּי־כֵן מֻתָּר לוֹ לְאָדָם לְהַחֲנִיף לָרְשָׁעִים מִפְּנֵי הַפַּחַד וּמִפְּנֵי הַיִּרְאָה שֶׁמִּתְיָרֵא אוֹ מְפַחֵד מִמֶּנּוּ.... וְכֵן יַעֲקֹב אָבִינוּ עָלָיו הַשָּׁלוֹם הֶחֱנִיף לְעֵשָׂו, שֶׁאָמַר לוֹ, כִּי עַל־כֵּן רָאִיתִי פָנֶיךָ כִּרְאֹת פְּנֵי אֱלֹהִים וַתִּרְצֵנִי.

Commentary

When Abram was ninety-nine years old, God appeared to him and said, "I am the Almighty God. Walk before Me and be *tamim*." (Genesis. 17:1) This episode precedes the first circumcision, a sign of the eternal covenant between God and the people of Israel. Being *tamim* is also the prerequisite for Abram's becoming Abraham—"father of a multitude"—a transformation that is related as much to Abraham's character and responsibility as it is to his name.

The word *tamim* has been translated into words such as "blameless," "perfect," and "whole-hearted." Despite the lack of a definitive English translation, it is clear that the virtue of *temimut* is related to the notion of personal integrity. Yechiel claims that God chooses the service of the person who acts with *temimut*. It is not enough just to "serve" God, whether through sacrifice or prayer. In addition to outer behavior, one must also possess the inner integrity that warrants divine acceptance.

Yechiel offers his own definition of *temimut*: The person who exhibits *temimut* is one who does not lie or cheat, whose "mouth and heart are equal." Yechiel connects *temimut* to ethics and argues that it represents the synthesis of both outer action and inner intention. The person whose word is gold (in private and in business matters) is the person who speaks the truth and does what he or she promises. Yet *temimut* is about more than just trustworthiness. It is also about wholeness. To be *tamim* is to integrate one's acts with one's soul so that behavior and desire become a single totality.

The virtue of *temimut* results in two fundamental benefits for the person who possesses it. First, that person will be "wanted" by God, who will take delight in him or her. As a result, the person who acts with *temimut* toward God and others will receive divine protection from sin. Second, *temimut* will "straighten the ways" for a person, smoothing out life's difficult paths and offering peace of mind and serenity. In both instances, *temimut* provides the shelter from the storm that we all crave.

Yechiel then turns his attention to the concept of *rama'ut*—"deceitfulness" and "hypocrisy"—the opposite of *temimut*. By using the story of the spies who were sent to assess the safety of *Eretz Yisrael* while the Israelites were still in the desert, Yechiel illustrates just how grave the consequences of *rama'ut* can be. The lies the spies told about the land of Canaan resulted in a spiritual death sentence for the bulk of their people. Only those Israelites who were under the age of twenty survived the desert wanderings and entered the Promised Land.

Deceitfulness and dishonesty are despised by God. If truth is one of the thirteen divine attributes, as we see from the text, then the person who lies absents himself or herself from contact with God's presence. Or, as punishment, God will hide God's presence from that person. Either way, the liar is left in the most profound and dire state of existential loneliness, whether as a result of his or her own (mis)behavior or as a consequence of God's "turning away," *hester panim*, from those who are not truthful—the worst kind of punishment imaginable.

There are instances, however, when deceitful behavior and the telling of lies are actually permitted. We are allowed to deceive and lie to the wicked of the world. Unlike the philosopher Immanuel Kant, who through his idea of the "categorical imperative" argues that if we are to be truthful we must be so at all times and in all situations, Yechiel implies that some contexts demand just the opposite. When Jacob confronted his brother Esau, for instance, he lied to him through flattery (according to Yechiel's interpretation of the verse) in order to cool Esau's anger and survive the encounter.

TEMIMUT IN JEWISH THOUGHT

The Maharal, Judah Loew of Prague, begins his discussion of the virtue of *temimut* by first distinguishing it from a similar virtue, that of *yosher*—"uprightness." He writes that

> the difference between them is that *yosher* derives from one's intellect and wisdom. One reflects [and then decides] to act with *yosher*. One who has integrity is the person who walks the way of *yosher* innately, without any contemplation.[1]

The fundamental distinction between *yosher* and *temimut* is cognitive. To be an upright person is clearly a Jewish virtue, but it is the result of deliberate thinking, of reflection and contemplation. After turning one's thoughts to a particular moral issue, one resolves to act in this or that way.

The person who possesses *temimut* acts not as a consequence of reflection but from reflex. Whether this attribute is the result of nature or nurture is not discussed. What matters is that the Jew who has integrity acts without thought, instinctively. Perhaps one of the clearest examples of *temimut* is the person who leaps into a surging river in order to save another from drowning without taking time to think about his or her safety or any other dilemma.

To possess *temimut* benefits a person in two ways. First, it frees a person from his or her sins, and second, it grants that person a kind of eternal life. The Maharal writes that "when a person [of integrity] is with God, those desires [that seek] to control him or her immediately leave the person."[2] The desires that lead to a life of sin are no match for the power of *temimut*.

Yet the virtue of *temimut* trancends the moral plane. The Maharal continues: "When that person is with God, he or she receives eternal life from God."[3] In the context of Jewish mysticism, which seems to be the one in which the Maharal is operating here, "eternal life" should be understood in its narrower, more technical sense: It is the ecstasy of *unio mystica*—the "mystical encounter." The Maharal links *temimut* with the kabbalistic idea of *devekut*—spiritual "adhesion" to God. Both phenomena, he writes, bring "eternal life" to the person who possesses or experiences them.

TEMIMUT IN JEWISH MYSTICISM

Rabbi Zaddok ha-Kohen, introduced in Chapter 3, discusses many spiritual virtues. His analysis of *temimut* stands out not only as particularly interesting but also as a little surprising. He writes:

> The fool is like a person with integrity [*tam*] in that he does not know [how] to deceive, since his mouth and his heart are equal. The person with integrity is better, for foolishness is sometimes necessary from him in order to serve God.[4]

In this startling comparison, Zaddok seems to equate the person who possesses *temimut* with the fool. This analogy is rooted in the fact that a person without sense would not know how to deceive even if he or she wanted to, since, as Yechiel argues, his or her "mouth and heart are equal." But while the fool acts with uprightness because of ignorance, the *tam* does so as the result of some inner harmony. The border between folly and integrity seems, at least in this interpretation, minute indeed.

Zaddok, however, claims that the folly of the *tam* is "better" than that of the fool because it is sometimes required for the service of God. The notion of serving God through the most mundane, even "foolish" acts, like drinking or dancing, is common in chasidic thought. Although many people might consider these acts to be foolish, they are, nevertheless, sincere attempts to connect with God. The fool is like the *tam* as a result of nature; the *tam* is like the fool as a result of context.

For Zaddok ha-Kohen, *temimut* is, in fact, the opposite of wisdom. Wisdom, conventionally understood, is a kind of knowledge that we acquire through our own experiences and efforts. According to Zaddok, the person who has *temimut* recognizes that ultimately everything, even knowledge, comes from God. That is spiritual wisdom. It is not something that we acquire or create. Rather, it is something that we *receive*.

Temimut: A Case Study

The notion of personal integrity is a central feature in Yechiel's spiritual system. In general, the person who possesses *temimut* is honest and free of deceit. Yet, as we have seen, situations in which lying is permitted do exist.

A TIME TO DECEIVE

Jennifer is a close friend of both Darcy and David, who are married. Soon after the couple's wedding, problems developed between them that have grown more and more pronounced over the past few weeks. Jennifer has become worried about Darcy. Lately, David's behavior toward Darcy has frequently been hostile and has sometimes even been aggressive. When Jennifer dis-

cussed the situation with David and asked what was wrong, he said everything was fine and that she should mind her own business. Darcy has consistently denied that there is a problem and says that she still loves David.

But today Darcy unexpectedly showed up at Jennifer's apartment. She had a black eye, a fat lip, and cuts over parts of her face. She told Jennifer that David had beaten her when he came home from work and that she needed a place to hide from him. She didn't want to call the police, but she also didn't know what to do. Jennifer cleaned Darcy's wounds and put her to bed. An hour later, David pounded on Jennifer's door, looking for Darcy. He was drunk and furious. After Jennifer refused to let him in, he calmed down, told her how much he loves Darcy, and said that he was going to get help. He asked if she knew where Darcy was.

——— WHAT SHOULD JENNIFER DO? ———

QUESTIONS FOR DISCUSSION

1. What issues must Jennifer weigh before making a decision?

2. Since both David and Darcy are her friends, how can Jennifer deal with her obligations to each of them when what one wants seems to conflict with what the other wants?

3. David says that he will change and insists that he poses no threat to Darcy. Should Jennifer believe him and tell him where Darcy is, or should she follow Darcy's wish to remain hidden from David for the time being?

4. What price might Jennifer have to pay for telling David the truth? For lying to him?

5. Do you think truthfulness, which is a moral good, is an absolute principle? Might it sometimes be sacrificed for the sake of another moral good? Which one(s)? Why?

6. Is it possible to be both a liar and a person who possesses *temimut*, one whose "mouth and heart are equal"? If so, how?

---

[1] *Netivot Olam*, vol. 2, 24:1
[2] Ibid.
[3] Ibid.
[4] *Kitvei Rabbi Zaddok ha-Kohen, Temimut*

Shem Tov
שֵׁם־טוֹב

My students, come and I will teach you about the virtue of a good name. Know, my students, that the virtue of a good name [*shem tov*] will come to a person as a result of works in service to God and that this is a very dear virtue and is only found in the pious and people of accomplishment and those who fear God in their service of God. Their good name travels far and wide. And even the Holy One went around to establish a good name in God's universe. As it is written: "Who is like Your people Israel, a unique nation on earth, whom God went and redeemed as God's people, winning renown for Godself and doing great and marvelous deeds for them?" [II Samuel 7:23] And our sages, of blessed memory, said in an *aggadah*: "We find that the Holy One, who is blessed, walked a journey of five hundred years in order to acquire a name in the universe. As it is written, 'Whom God went and redeemed.' [II Samuel 7:23] Thus from the earth to the firmament, the journey is five hundred years." [*Kohelet Rabbah* 7:2]

בָּנַי, בֹּאוּ וַאֲלַמֶּדְכֶם מַעֲלַת שֵׁם־טוֹב. דְּעוּ בָנַי, כִּי מַעֲלַת שֵׁם־טוֹב שֶׁיֵּצֵא לוֹ לְאָדָם בְּמַעֲשֵׂה עֲבוֹדַת הָאֱלֹהִים, הִיא מַעֲלָה יְקָרָה, וְאֵינָהּ נִמְצֵאת אֶלָּא בַּחֲסִידִים וְאַנְשֵׁי מַעֲשֶׂה וְיִרְאֵי הָאֵל אֲשֶׁר בַּעֲבוֹדָתָם אֶת הָאֱלֹהִים, שְׁמָם הַטּוֹב הוֹלֵךְ לְמֵרָחוֹק. וַאֲפִילוּ הַקָּדוֹשׁ־בָּרוּךְ־הוּא בְּעַצְמוֹ חָזַר לִקְנוֹת שֵׁם־טוֹב בְּעוֹלָמוֹ, שֶׁנֶּאֱמַר, אֲשֶׁר־הָלְכוּ אֱלֹהִים לִפְדּוֹת־לוֹ וְגוֹ'. וְאָמְרוּ חֲכָמֵינוּ זִכְרוֹנָם לִבְרָכָה בָּאַגָּדָה, מָצִינוּ שֶׁהָלַךְ הַקָּדוֹשׁ־בָּרוּךְ־הוּא מַהֲלַךְ חֲמֵשׁ־מֵאוֹת שָׁנָה לִקְנוֹת לוֹ שֵׁם בְּעוֹלָמוֹ, שֶׁנֶּאֱמַר, אֲשֶׁר הָלְכוּ־אֱלֹהִים לִפְדּוֹת־לוֹ וְגוֹ'. שֶׁכֵּן מִן הָאָרֶץ עַד לָרָקִיעַ מַהֲלַךְ חֲמֵשׁ־מֵאוֹת שָׁנָה.

A good name is worth more than all the silver and gold that is in the world. As it is written: "Repute is preferable to great wealth; good grace is better than silver and gold." [Proverbs 22:1]

My students, strive to acquire a good

גְּדוֹלָה מַעֲלַת שֵׁם־טוֹב יוֹתֵר מִכָּל כֶּסֶף וְזָהָב שֶׁבָּעוֹלָם, כָּעִנְיָן שֶׁנֶּאֱמַר, נִבְחָר שֵׁם מֵעשֶׁר רָב מִכֶּסֶף וּמִזָּהָב חֵן טוֹב. בָּנַי, הִשְׁתַּדְּלוּ לִקְנוֹת שֵׁם־טוֹב בָּעוֹלָם אֲשֶׁר אַתֶּם עוֹמְדִין בּוֹ, בְּיִרְאַת־שָׁמַיִם,

name in the world that you inhabit, with fear of heaven and in the service of God and with love of all creatures, because the good name will be your witness in this world and in the World to Come. And the good name is the greatest attribute/pedigree [*gadol shebayechasim*]. As one sage put it: "The greatest attribute is the good name. And there is no better way of separating oneself from evil desires [as a way of acquiring a good name] than the closing of one's eyes." [*Mivchar Hapeninim* 14:1] Another sage said: "An attribute of the dear of soul is that a person will be concerned with the way in which he will be remembered and that he will acquire a good name and trust in God—that is perfect faith." [*Mivchar Hapeninim* 14:4]

The virtue of a good name is beloved and especially on the day of death. As it is written: "A good name is better than fine oil, and the day of death [is better] than the day of birth." [Ecclesiastes 7:1] And our sages, of blessed memory, said in an *aggadah*: "A person is called by three names: the one that his parents gave to him, the one that he calls himself, and the one the Holy One, who is blessed, uses in the book of generations. As it is written: 'This is the book of the generations of humanity [*adam*].' [Genesis 5:1] And what is he called? Adam. But you do not know which of them [the names] is more beloved. Solomon came and explained, 'Better is the name that is used on the day of death than the name used on the day of birth.' [Ecclesiastes 7:1] For at the time that the Holy One said to Moses, 'Appoint for Me a High Priest,' Moses said to God, 'From which tribe should he be?' God said, 'From the tribe of Levi.' At that time, Moses was happy and said, 'How beloved is my tribe!' The Holy One said to him, 'The names of the tribes are dearer to Me than the anoint-

וּבַעֲבוֹדַת־הַמָּקוֹם, וְאַהֲבַת־הַבְּרִיּוֹת, מִפְּנֵי שֶׁהַשֵּׁם־טוֹב יְעִידְךָ בָּעוֹלָם הַזֶּה וְלָעוֹלָם הַבָּא. וְהַשֵּׁם־טוֹב הוּא הַגָּדוֹל שֶׁבַּיְחָסִים, כְּמוֹ שֶׁאָמַר חָכָם אֶחָד, הַגָּדוֹל שֶׁבַּיְחָסִים, הַשֵּׁם־הַטּוֹב. וְאֵין חוֹצֵץ בִּפְנֵי הַתַּאֲווֹת כַּעֲצִימַת הָעֵינַיִם. וְאָמַר אַחֵר, מִיקַּר־ הַנֶּפֶשׁ, שֶׁיָּחוּשׁ הָאָדָם עַל זִכְרוֹ וְשֶׁיִּקְנֶה הַשֵּׁם הַטּוֹב וְיִבְטַח בֵּאלֹהִים, הִיא הָאֱמוּנָה הַגְּמוּרָה.

חֲבִיבָה מַעֲלַת שֵׁם־טוֹב וּבְיוֹתֵר בְּיוֹם הַמִּיתָה, כָּעִנְיָן שֶׁנֶּאֱמַר, טוֹב שֵׁם מִשֶּׁמֶן טוֹב וְיוֹם הַמָּוֶת מִיּוֹם הִוָּלְדוֹ. וְאָמְרוּ חֲכָמֵינוּ זִכְרוֹנָם לִבְרָכָה בָּאַגָּדָה, שְׁלֹשָׁה שֵׁמוֹת נִקְרְאוּ לוֹ לְאָדָם, אֶחָד שֶׁקָּרְאוּ לוֹ אָבִיו וְאִמּוֹ, וְאֶחָד שֶׁקּוֹרֵא לוֹ הוּא בְּעַצְמוֹ, וְאֶחָד שֶׁקָּרָא לוֹ הַקָּדוֹשׁ־בָּרוּךְ־הוּא בְּסֵפֶר תּוֹלְדוֹת, שֶׁנֶּאֱמַר, זֶה סֵפֶר תּוֹלְדֹת אָדָם וְגוֹ'. וּמַה קּוֹרֵא אוֹתוֹ? אָדָם. אֲבָל אֵין אַתָּה יוֹדֵעַ אֵיזֶה מֵהֶן חָבִיב. בָּא שְׁלֹמֹה וּפֵרַשׁ, טוֹב שֵׁם – שֶׁבְּיוֹם הַמָּוֶת, מִיּוֹם הִוָּלְדוֹ. שֶׁבְּשָׁעָה שֶׁאָמַר לוֹ הַקָּדוֹשׁ־בָּרוּךְ־ הוּא לְמֹשֶׁה מַנֵּה לִי כֹּהֵן־גָּדוֹל, אָמַר לוֹ מֹשֶׁה, מֵאֵיזֶה שֵׁבֶט יִתְמַנֶּה? אָמַר לוֹ, מִשִּׁבְטוֹ שֶׁל לֵוִי. בְּאוֹתָהּ שָׁעָה, שָׂמַח מֹשֶׁה וְאָמַר, כָּךְ שִׁבְטִי חָבִיב! אָמַר לוֹ הַקָּדוֹשׁ־בָּרוּךְ־הוּא, חֲבִיבִין עָלַי שְׁמוֹתֵיהֶן שֶׁל שְׁבָטִים מִשֶּׁמֶן־הַמִּשְׁחָה שֶׁכֹּהֵן־גָּדוֹל נִמְשָׁח בּוֹ. שֶׁאֵין עֲבוֹדָתוֹ שֶׁל כֹּהֵן־גָּדוֹל עֲבוֹדָה וְאֵינוֹ נִכְנָס לְכַפֵּר, אֲלוּלֵי שְׁמוֹתֵיהֶן שֶׁל שְׁבָטִים נְתוּנִין עַל לִבּוֹ. וַאֲפִילוּ הָיוּ חֲסֵרִין אוֹת אַחַת אוֹ נְקֻדָה אַחַת, לֹא הָיָה נִכְנָס כֹּהֵן לְכַפֵּר, שֶׁנֶּאֱמַר, שִׁשָּׁה מִשְּׁמֹתָם עַל הָאֶבֶן הָאֶחָת וְגוֹ' – שֶׁיְּהֵא שְׁמָם תָּם. בְּשָׁעָה שֶׁהָיוּ חַיִּים, לֹא

ing oil that the High Priest uses to anoint himself.' For the service of the High Priest is no service and he does not enter to gain atonement if the names of the tribes are not placed over his heart. And if even one letter or one vowel was missing [from these names], the High Priest would not enter to gain atonement. As it is written: 'Six of their names will be on the one stone' [Exodus 28:10] so that their names will be whole. At the time that they [the tribes] were living, they did not merit to hear this. But once they were dead, it was written, 'six of their names.'" [*Midrash Samuel* 23:6, *Ecclesiastes Rabbah* 7:3-4]

זָכוּ לִשְׁמוֹעַ דָּבָר זֶה. וּבְשָׁעָה שֶׁמֵּתוּ, כְּתִיב שִׁשָּׁה מִשְּׁמוֹתָם.

My students, desire a good name in the service of God and out of love for all creatures, for the honor of heaven and not for your own honor, and not in order to achieve authority in the world, as the fools do, who desire a good name in the world for their own honor, for vanity in the world and not for the honor of heaven.

בָּנַי, תִּתְאַווּ לְשֵׁם־טוֹב בַּעֲבוֹדַת הַמָּקוֹם וְאַהֲבַת כָּל הַבְּרִיּוֹת לִכְבוֹד שָׁמַיִם, לֹא לִכְבוֹד עַצְמְכֶם וְלֹא לְשֵׁם שְׂרָרָה בָּעוֹלָם כַּאֲשֶׁר יַעֲשׂוּ הַסְּכָלִים הַמִּתְאַוִּים לִקְנוֹת שֵׁם־טוֹב בָּעוֹלָם לִכְבוֹד עַצְמָם בְּהַבְלֵי־ הָעוֹלָם וְלֹא לִכְבוֹד שָׁמַיִם.

Commentary

When we hear that someone has a good name, we oftentimes associate that person with a whole set of positive attributes: trustworthiness, honesty, reliability, and a good moral character. The virtue of a *shem tov*—"good name"—is also valued in the Jewish tradition. As the Book of Proverbs 22:1 states, "Repute is preferable to great wealth." In Yechiel's spiritual system, the virtue of a *shem tov* is treated with equal respect, although we shall see that its value and definition go far beyond any ordinary, everyday understanding of the term.

The virtue of a good name will come to a person only as the consequence of one thing—service to God. It is not other people who ultimately bestow upon a person the honor of being a *shem tov*. It is God. One reaches this spiritual level not via secular achievements or honors but through great piety and the fear of God in one's heart and soul. As Yechiel notes, the virtue of a good name "travels far and wide." No matter how hard we work at trying to earn such an honor, in the end it is beyond our grasp and transcends our control. Our colleagues and peers are powerless to give it to us. God alone can grant us this gift and coronate us with a *keter shem tov*—a "crown of a good name."

Just as human beings strive to make a good name for themselves, so God strives to give God a good name. But while God alone can bestow such a virtue on us, it is the universe that can bestow this virtue on God. God must impress the world and its creatures before they will bow down and grant God the title of a *shem tov*. Thus all of the supernatural wonders, miracles, and marvels that God inserted into the natural world (e.g., the parting of the Sea of Reeds and the pillars of smoke and fire) are viewed as testimonies to God's power and expressions of God's benificence in order to win us over. The implications are startling: God needs our approval as much as we need God's.

The virtue of a good name is more valuable than all of the world's riches. Anything that is made of matter, such as coins, clothing, and flesh, is susceptible to the force of time and is, therefore, in a constant state of atrophy and disintegration. Only that which is spiritual, like the virtue of a *shem tov*, is free from decay and of lasting value. A good name not only endures beyond death; it also grants its possessor eternal life in the World to Come. For this reason, it is viewed by some sages as the greatest of all the spiritual attributes.

The virtue of a *shem tov* is even more precious on the day of one's death. Why? Because to live is to exist in time, and to exist in time, as we noted above, entails change. It is possible for a person to forfeit or lose the gift of a good name during his or her lifetime. We all sin. We all make mistakes. And we sometimes do things that are evil. The virtue of a *shem tov* is as impermanent as life itself—impermanent, that is, until the day of death. At that point, our deeds are completed and our characters fixed for all time, never to change. If we have merited the crown of a good name, it is ours to keep.

Every single one of us is called by many names. Our parents call us by one name, our friends by another, and our spouses by still another. We even refer to ourselves in terms different from those used by the rest of the world. We all have many *selves*. Postmodernism has shown us that human beings present countless names or faces to the world and to ourselves and that those faces change depending on time and context. Am I the same person now that I was at age five? Am I Dr. Schwartz in the morning but Dave or Dad at night? It is only after death concretizes our personalities that the value of a good name becomes truly clear.

The motivation for wanting a good name should be the desire to serve God and love for all God's creatures. If the impetus for righteous behavior is the desire for some external gain, like power, wealth, or fame—all forms of selfishness and self-aggrandizement—then all our good deeds become spiritually worthless. Rather than honoring God, such a motivation profanes God's world and is an abomination in God's sight. The surest way for a person to bring honor to himself or herself, to crown himself or herself with a *keter shem tov*, is to *disregard* himself or herself. The virtue of a good name belongs to the selfless, to the God-fearers, to those who devote their lives and efforts not to themselves but to their Creator and Redeemer.

SHEM TOV IN JEWISH THOUGHT

Judah Loew, the Maharal, discusses the virtue of a *shem tov* at the end of his book *Netivot Olam*. For the Maharal, the acquisition of a good name is one of the final "paths," *netivot*, on our spiritual journey. Although a discussion of this virtue appears at the very end of the Maharal's work and receives only a few pages of commentary, the virtue of a *shem tov* is an integral part of his spiritual system and is cited by him as one of very few inner virtues that go with the person who possesses them into the world beyond.

The Maharal writes:

> "A good name is better than fine oil." [*Kohelet* 7:1] What is the rela-
> tion between a "good name" [*shem tov*] and "fine oil" [*shemen tov*]?
> Neither has any [apparent] connection to the other, except for the
> similarity that a good name emits a "fragrance" that can be detected
> from a distance, and, even more than strong spices, can [overpower]
> the smell of fine oil.[1]

In addition to the obvious wordplay between *shem tov* and *shemen tov*, the Maharal finds a more tangible relationship between these two seemingly disparate items. The virtue of a good name, according to the Maharal, has an almost *palpable* quality: Like oil—presumably olive oil, which has a powerful smell—a *shem tov* somehow radiates or emanates a "fragrance" to the world. Just how this fragrance enters the concrete world and what its odor resembles are unexplained. The Maharal only appears to suggest that the Jew who wears a *keter shem tov* radiates a kind of *spiritual aura*—an aura that is as palpable and pleasant to the outside world as a perfume.

The difference between *shem tov* and *shemen tov* is that the fragrance of the former will last forever. The Maharal continues:

> When life departs from a man, so, too, does any degree or honor that
> he has received depart from him. Clearly [things like] power and
> wealth no longer belong to him when he is dead. Yet a good name,

since it is his abstract essence, is not related to death at all, for the crown of a good name is even greater than the crown of the Torah. Thus a good name, which guides a person's rational nature and transcends his material nature, is not at all connected to death.[2]

After a person dies, all those external things that he or she possessed during life, like titles, awards, power, and riches, are lost to him or her for eternity. Our material possessions simply do not and cannot follow us to the grave. However, a *shem tov*, which is related to the spiritual rather than the physical part of a human being, can and does pass through the gateway into *Olam Haba*—the "World to Come." Only a person's physical body perishes. The glory of a good name outlives a person's body because it is not in any way connected to the realm of matter. It is not a title but a strand of one's soul.

The Maharal states that a *keter shem tov* is even greater than the crown of the Torah. This is a striking idea in light of the high value Judaism places on Scripture. But this notion predates the Maharal by many centuries. In *Pirkei Avot*, for instance, we find perhaps the most famous reference to the *keter shem tov*:

> Rabbi Simeon said: "There are three crowns—the crown of Torah, the crown of the priesthood, and the crown of royalty. But the crown of a good name surpasses them all."[3]

As great a value as religious learning is, it, like prestige and power, cannot last beyond the moment of death. A *keter shem tov*, however, which is purely spiritual in nature and, therefore, unrelated to the material world, will not perish along with a person's body. It is the crown of all crowns.

SHEM TOV IN JEWISH MYSTICISM

Rabbi Zaddok ha-Kohen also views a good name as a virtue that has intimate and exclusive connections to a person's soul. For Zaddok, a *shem tov* is a spiritual reality that transcends this world and carries over into the world beyond. Commenting on the verse "A good name is better than fine oil" from the book of *Kohelet*, Zaddok argues that a *shem tov*, which is something holy, is "everlasting" and is immune to the forces of time.[4]

Zaddok continues:

> A good name alludes to the purification of the soul. An illustration is the day of death, when the soul separates from the body and no longer needs to perform the commandments—which are hinted at through the words "fine oil."[5]

When a person is alive, the soul is encased in and animates the body. As a result, the soul becomes susceptible to contamination from the damage of physical pollutants—like forbidden foods—and the stain of moral ones—like sins and transgressions. On the other hand, a *shem tov* suggests spiritual purification because it is a reality that lasts beyond the life span of the body. At the moment of death, the soul separates from the body and becomes an independent essence. Since it is no longer "human," it is no longer required to perform the *mitzvot* (represented by the image of "fine oil") that are the obligations of all Jews, which are designed to make us more spiritually pure beings. A good name, which is linked to the soul, is *already* pure and beyond the reach of physical impurities and moral pollution.

Zaddok expands on the subject of names:

> There are two types of names, as we learn from the Book of Genesis: "She shall be called Woman [*isha*] because she was taken out of Man [*ish*]" (2:23), and "The man called his wife's name Eve [*Chavah*] because she was the mother of all the living [*chai*]." (3:20) The first type is a public name, and this name refers to one's beginning and cause—where one was "taken" from. The second type is a private name, and this refers to one's final end and for what [purpose] one has been designed.[6]

In this fascinating interpretation, Zaddok finds significant meaning in the two different names assigned to Eve, the primeval woman. She is first referred to as *isha*, since it was from the rib of *ish*—"man"—that she was taken. The name *isha* is her general, public name, the name that *identifies* her. In identifying the woman, it tells us about her origin, where she came from, her beginning. This is the name by which the world calls her, the name *ish* called her at the moment when she came into being.

The second name is more intimate, more personal. The name *Chavah* does not refer to the woman's origin and does not relate to the man in any way. Rather, it is a private name that refers to her *identity*, as opposed to her identification. The name *Chavah* tells us not where she is from but who she *is*. It describes her character and personality, her function and purpose. It is more than just a reference to the woman's origins. The name *Chavah* informs us of her destiny as the "mother of all the living." We can only assume that a *shem tov* is a third, even higher kind of name, and a name by which only a select few ever come to be called.

Shem Tov: A Case Study

The term *shem tov* is difficult to define. Certain general characteristics, however, such as a life devoted to the service of God, appear to be essential components to the process of acquiring a good name. It would seem inappropriate, for instance, to view someone who did not live a profoundly ethical or compassionate life as a representative of this virtue. The difficulty stems from the fact that there are many different ways to be a good person and that simply being good does not necessarily warrant the honor that a *keter shem tov* confers.

TWO GOOD PEOPLE

Amy is a young woman who has chosen to dedicate her life to others. She joined the Peace Corps after college and taught English in central Africa for three years. Upon returning to the United States, she concluded that Western values were empty and bankrupt and decided to pursue a life of simplicity and altruisim. She lives alone in a small, stark apartment in the inner city, has almost no possessions, and spends her time working with the poor, infirm, and elderly. Her commitment to others is total. Amy feels that friends and family would distract her from her mission, which brings her deep spiritual fulfillment.

Ebenezer is a family man, a hard worker who does everything for his wife and their two young children. He is a good person and is not at all materialistic, although he has not renounced the material world. On the contrary, his motivation to work hard stems from his desire to provide for his family's needs, which include a nice house, a comfortable life-style, and a good education for their children. On Shabbat, Ebenezer always stays home from work and tries to take his family to services at their local synagogue whenever he can. While by no means an extremist, Ebenezer views his family as the most important entity in his life.

— WHICH PERSON MIGHT POSSESS A SHEM TOV? —

QUESTIONS FOR DISCUSSION

1. In what ways is Amy a good, ethical person? What about Ebenezer?

2. Does ethical behavior alone earn a person the title of a good name? What else might be needed?

3. Are there any aspects of Amy's or Ebenezer's life or life-style that you would consider spiritually unfulfilling? Which ones? Why?

4. If being crowned with a *keter shem tov* is ultimately about serving God, what do you think constitutes divine service? Why?

5. Which of these two people do you think "serves God" more truly?

6. Are worldly values like taking care of one's family and spiritual values mutually exclusive? Might the two sometimes be identical? Why or why not?

---

[1] *Netivot Olam*, vol. 2, 32:1
[2] Ibid.
[3] *Pirkei Avot* 4:17
[4] *Kitvei Rabbi Zaddok ha-Kohen, Shem Tov*
[5] Ibid.
[6] Ibid.

Teshuvah

תְּשׁוּבָה

Come, my students, and I will instruct you in the virtue of repentance. Know, my students, that the virtue of repentance [*teshuvah*] is very great. Because of its importance, the Holy One made it precede the creation of the world. As it is written: "Before the mountains came into being, before You brought forth the earth and the world, from eternity to eternity, You are God." [Psalms 90:2] And right after that verse it is written: *Tashev enosh ad daka*—"You return man to contrition, and you decree, 'Return, you mortals.'"[Psalms 90:3] And not only that, but this [repentance] touches the throne of glory. As it is written: *Shuvah Yisrael*— "Return, O Israel, to your God." [Hosea 14:2]

And our sages, of blessed memory, said in an *aggadah* [Pesikta Rabbati, Chapter 44]: "So great is the power of *teshuvah* that as soon as a person thinks in his heart of doing *teshuvah*, it immediately ascends upward. And you should not say for only ten *mil* or for only twenty *mil* or for only one hundred *mil*. Rather, it goes on for the distance of five hundred years. And not only to the first firmament, not only to the second firmament, but rather it ascends until it stands before the throne of glory." As it is written: "Return, O Israel, to your God." [Hosea 14:2]

בָּנַי, בֹּאוּ וַאֲלַמֶּדְכֶם מַעֲלַת הַתְּשׁוּבָה. דְּעוּ בָּנַי, כִּי מַעֲלַת הַתְּשׁוּבָה, מַעֲלָה גְדוֹלָה עַד־מְאֹד. וּמִתּוֹךְ חֲשִׁיבוּתָהּ, קָדְמָה הַקָּדוֹשׁ־בָּרוּךְ־הוּא לִבְרִיאַת הָעוֹלָם, כָּעִנְיָן שֶׁנֶּאֱמַר, בְּטֶרֶם הָרִים יֻלָּדוּ וַתְּחוֹלֵל אֶרֶץ וְתֵבֵל וּמֵעוֹלָם עַד־עוֹלָם אַתָּה אֵל. וּכְתִיב בַּתְרֵהּ, תָּשֵׁב אֱנוֹשׁ עַד־דַּכָּא וַתֹּאמֶר שׁוּבוּ בְנֵי־אָדָם. וְלֹא עוֹד אֶלָּא, שֶׁמַּגַּעַת עַד כִּסֵּא־הַכָּבוֹד, כָּעִנְיָן שֶׁנֶּאֱמַר, שׁוּבָה יִשְׂרָאֵל עַד יְיָ אֱלֹהֶיךָ וְגוֹ'.

וְאָמְרוּ חֲכָמֵינוּ זִכְרוֹנָם לִבְרָכָה בָּאַגָּדָה, גָּדוֹל כֹּחָהּ שֶׁל תְּשׁוּבָה, שֶׁכֵּיוָן שֶׁאָדָם מְהַרְהֵר בְּלִבּוֹ לַעֲשׂוֹת תְּשׁוּבָה, מִיָּד הִיא עוֹלָה לְמַעְלָה. וְלֹא תֹאמַר עַד עֲשָׂרָה מִילִין אוֹ עַד עֶשְׂרִים אוֹ עַד מֵאָה מִילִין, אֶלָּא עַד מַהֲלַךְ חֲמֵשׁ מֵאוֹת שָׁנָה. וְלֹא עַד רָקִיעַ הָרִאשׁוֹן וְלֹא עַד רָקִיעַ הַשֵּׁנִי, אֶלָּא עַד שֶׁהִיא עוֹלָה וְעוֹמֶדֶת לִפְנֵי כִסֵּא־הַכָּבוֹד, שֶׁנֶּאֱמַר, שׁוּבָה יִשְׂרָאֵל עַד יְיָ אֱלֹהֶיךָ וְגוֹ'.

Teshuvah is great. Even if a person was thoroughly evil all his life and then did complete *teshuvah*, at the end of his days the Holy One does not remind him of any of his transgressions that he committed in the beginning. As it is written: "The former things shall not be remembered and they shall never come to mind." [Isaiah 65:17] And not only that, but *teshuvah* is greater than the sacrificial offerings. As it is written: "Surely obedience is better than a good sacrifice, and compliance [is better] than the fat of rams." [I Samuel 15:22]

גְּדוֹלָה הִיא הַתְּשׁוּבָה. שֶׁאֲפִילוּ אִם הָיָה רָשָׁע גָּמוּר כָּל יָמָיו וְעָשָׂה תְּשׁוּבָה שְׁלֵמָה בְּסוֹף יָמָיו, אֵין הַקָּדוֹשׁ־בָּרוּךְ־הוּא מַזְכִּיר לוֹ כְּלוּם מֵעֲוֹנוֹתָיו אֲשֶׁר עָשָׂה מִתְּחִלָּה, שֶׁנֶּאֱמַר, וְלֹא תִזָּכַרְנָה הָרִאשֹׁנוֹת וְלֹא תַעֲלֶינָה עַל־לֵב. וְלֹא עוֹד אֶלָּא שֶׁהַתְּשׁוּבָה גְּדוֹלָה יוֹתֵר מִן הַקָּרְבָּנוֹת, שֶׁנֶּאֱמַר, הִנֵּה שְׁמֹעַ מִזֶּבַח טוֹב לְהַקְשִׁיב מֵחֵלֶב אֵילִים.

And what is *teshuvah*? And in what manner [how] does a person return to the Creator? After a person knows that he has sinned and knows the offensiveness and shamefulness of his acts, he should overcome his evil inclination and battle with it, and he should try to overcome his desire and force his spirit to remove itself from the beastly desires and vanities of this world. And he should calculate for himself the momentary sweetness of the transgressions compared to its bitterness and the loss to his soul of the World to Come. Let him always think to himself of the transgressions he has committed, and they should always be before his eyes. As it is written: "For I recognize my transgressions and am ever conscious of my sin." [Psalms 51:5] And he should be in awe of the Creator and humbled before God, and he should think to himself against whom he has rebelled, and he should regret his iniquities and not repeat them, and he should ask pardon from the Creator for the rest of his days so that God will accept him and so that the Holy One will pardon him for all his

וּמַה הִיא הַתְּשׁוּבָה, וּבְאֵיזֶה עִנְיָן יָשׁוּב הָאָדָם לְבוֹרְאוֹ? אַחַר שֶׁיֵּדַע הָאָדָם שֶׁחָטָא וְיוֹדֵעַ גְּנוּת מַעֲשָׂיו וְחֶרְפָּתָם, יְהֵא מִתְגַּבֵּר עַל יִצְרוֹ וְנִלְחָם עִמּוֹ, וְיִשְׁתַּדֵּל לְהַכְנִיעַ תַּאֲוָתוֹ וּלְהַכְרִיחַ נַפְשׁוֹ לְהָסִירָהּ מִתַּאֲווֹת הַבַּהֲמִיּוֹת וְהַבְלֵי הָעוֹלָם הַזֶּה. וְיַחֲשֹׁב בְּעַצְמוֹ מְתִיקוּת הָעֲבֵרָה לְפִי שָׁעָה, כְּנֶגֶד מְרִירוּתָהּ וְאָבְדַן נַפְשׁוֹ מֵחַיֵּי הָעוֹלָם הַבָּא. וְיַתְמִיד לַחְשֹׁב בְּעַצְמוֹ עַל הָעֲבֵרוֹת שֶׁעָשָׂה, וְיִהְיוּ נֶגֶד עֵינָיו תָּמִיד, כָּעִנְיָן שֶׁנֶּאֱמַר, כִּי־פְשָׁעַי אֲנִי אֵדָע וְחַטָּאתִי נֶגְדִּי תָמִיד. וְיִהְיֶה יָרֵא מִבּוֹרְאוֹ וְיֵבוֹשׁ מִמֶּנּוּ, וְיַחֲשֹׁב בְּעַצְמוֹ נֶגֶד מִי הִמְרָה, וְיִתְחָרֵט עַל עֲווֹנוֹתָיו וְלֹא יִשְׁנֶה עֲלֵיהֶם, וִיבַקֵּשׁ עֲלֵיהֶם מְחִילָה מֵאֵת הַבּוֹרֵא כָּל יְמֵי חַיָּיו, כְּדֵי שֶׁיְּקַבְּלֶנּוּ וְיִמְחוֹל לוֹ הַקָּדוֹשׁ־בָּרוּךְ־הוּא עַל כָּל עֲווֹנוֹתָיו. וְצָרִיךְ לוֹ לְבַעַל־תְּשׁוּבָה [לֵידַע] גְּנוּת מַעֲשָׂיו וְחֶרְפָּתָם עַל הַבֵּרוּר. כִּי, אִם יִסְתַּפֵּק לוֹ בָּהֶם, אִי־אֶפְשָׁר לוֹ לְהִתְחָרֵט עֲלֵיהֶם חֲרָטָה גְמוּרָה. וְכֵן צָרִיךְ לוֹ לֵידַע,

transgressions. And the person who repents [ba'al teshuvah] must know clearly the disgracefulness and shamefulness of his acts, because if he is in doubt about the ugliness of his sins, he cannot possibly have complete remorse for having done them. And he must also know that if he does not return to God with complete *teshuvah* from his sins and if he does not confess them, then God will punish him for his evil deeds.

שֶׁאִם לֹא יָשׁוּב בִּתְשׁוּבָה שְׁלֵמָה מֵחֲטָאָיו לִפְנֵי הַמָּקוֹם וְאֵינוֹ מִתְוַדֶּה עֲלֵיהֶן, שֶׁהַקָּדוֹשׁ־בָּרוּךְ־הוּא נִפְרָע מִמֶּנּוּ עַל מַעֲשָׂיו הָרָעִים.

And you must know, my students, that *teshuvah* is medication for sins and iniquities, just as bandages and other sorts of medications will heal wounds and injuries. And not only that, but also through *teshuvah* a person will become beloved to the Holy One where once the Holy One despised him because he pursued the desires of his heart and his eyes and went after his evil inclination. Thus we find that evildoers are called Haters of God. As it is written: "Who instantly requites with destruction those who reject God." [Deuteronomy 7:10] And thus it is written: "O God, You know that I hate those who hate You and quarrel with Your adversaries." [Psalms 139:21]

וּדְעוּ לָכֶם בָּנַי, כִּי הַתְּשׁוּבָה, רְפוּאָה עַל הַחֲטָאִים וְהָעֲוֹנוֹת כַּאֲשֶׁר הַתַּחְבֹּשֶׁת וּשְׁאָר מִינֵי הָרְפוּאוֹת רְפוּאָה אֶל הַנְּגָעִים וְהַמַּכּוֹת. וְלֹא עוֹד אֶלָּא, שֶׁבַּתְּשׁוּבָה יִהְיֶה הָאָדָם אָהוּב לְבוֹרְאוֹ תַּחַת אֲשֶׁר הָיָה הַקָּדוֹשׁ־בָּרוּךְ־הוּא שׂוֹנְאוֹ בְּלֶכְתּוֹ אַחַר תַּאֲוַת לִבּוֹ וְאַחַר מַרְאֵה עֵינָיו וְאַחַר יִצְרוֹ [הָרַע]. שֶׁכֵּן מָצִינוּ שֶׁהָרְשָׁעִים נִקְרָאִין שׂוֹנְאֵי־הַמָּקוֹם, כָּעִנְיָן שֶׁנֶּאֱמַר, וּמְשַׁלֵּם לְשׂנְאָיו אֶל־פָּנָיו לְהַאֲבִידוֹ. וְכֵן הוּא אוֹמֵר, הֲלוֹא־מְשַׂנְאֶיךָ, יְיָ, אֶשְׂנָא, וּבִתְקוֹמְמֶיךָ אֶתְקוֹטָט.

Therefore, my students, always knock on the gates of *teshuvah* with crying and with tears, for no one should impede a person who wishes to draw closer to God. Rather, the Holy One opens for him the good and upright path and clears the way for him and helps him with God's service and teaches him the good way with compassion and goodness. As it is written: "Good and upright is God. Therefore, God shows sin-

לָכֵן בָּנַי, דִּפְקוּ תָמִיד בְּשַׁעַר הַתְּשׁוּבָה בִּבְכִי וּבְדִמְעָה. שֶׁכָּל מִי שֶׁרוֹצֶה לְהִתְקָרֵב אֶל הָאֱלֹהִים, אֵין מִי שֶׁמּוֹנֵעַ אוֹתוֹ מִלְהִתְקָרֵב אֵלָיו, אֲבָל הַקָּדוֹשׁ־בָּרוּךְ־הוּא בְּעַצְמוֹ פּוֹתֵחַ לוֹ דֶּרֶךְ הַטּוֹבָה וְהַיְשָׁרָה, וּמְסַקֵּל לְפָנָיו הַמְסִלָּה, וּמְסַיְּעוֹ בְּמַעֲשֵׂה עֲבוֹדָתוֹ, וּמוֹרֶה אוֹתוֹ הַדֶּרֶךְ הַטּוֹבָה בְּחַסְדּוֹ וְטוֹבוֹ, כָּעִנְיָן שֶׁנֶּאֱמַר, טוֹב

ners the way." [Psalms 25:8] And it is written: "And if you search there [in exile] for your God, you will find God, but only if you seek the Eternal with all your heart and your soul." [Deuteronomy 4:29] And it is written: "God is near to all those who call, to all who call in truth." [Psalms 145:18] And the sages, of blessed memory, said: "One who comes to purify himself is aided from above." [*Shabbat* 104a] And our God with mercy will bring us back in full *teshuvah* for the sake of God's great compassion.

וְיָשָׁר יְיָ עַל־כֵּן יוֹרֶה חַטָּאִים בַּדָּרֶךְ. וְאוֹמֵר, וּבִקַּשְׁתֶּם מִשָּׁם אֶת־יְיָ אֱלֹהֶיךָ וּמָצָאתָ כִּי תִדְרְשֶׁנּוּ בְּכָל־לְבָבְךָ וּבְכָל־נַפְשֶׁךָ. וְכֵן הוּא אוֹמֵר, קָרוֹב יְיָ לְכָל־קֹרְאָיו לְכֹל אֲשֶׁר יִקְרָאֻהוּ בֶאֱמֶת. וְאָמְרוּ חֲכָמֵינוּ זִכְרוֹנָם לִבְרָכָה, בָּא לִטַּהֵר, מְסַיְּעִין אוֹתוֹ. וֵאלֹהֵינוּ בְּרַחֲמָיו יְשִׁיבֵנוּ בִתְשׁוּבָה שְׁלֵמָה לְפָנָיו לְמַעַן חֲסָדָיו הָרַבִּים.

Commentary

Most Jews associate the concept of *teshuvah* with the Days of Awe, the period known as the Ten Days of Repentance, which ends with Yom Kippur. This is the time of year when Jews turn inward, when our everyday concerns are temporarily suspended so that we may focus solely on matters of the spirit. If we have sinned, as all of us inevitably have, then this becomes our season for atonement, the time to ask God for forgiveness.

For Yechiel, however, the opportunities for *teshuvah* are not so limited nor its descriptions so narrow. As he points out, God made *teshuvah* precede even the creation of the world. If this is the case, then *teshuvah* represents a value that transcends time and space. It is an eternal value rather than one that is context-specific. *Teshuvah* is as much about the idea of return as it is about repentance. It is the gate through which we can reunite with our primeval Source.

The virtue of *teshuvah* will bring us to *kisei hakavod*—the "throne of glory." The earliest circles of Jewish mystics, whose spiritual system is often referred to as *Merkabah* mysticism, wrote frequently of "visions of the throne," their brushes with the Godhead. Although Yechiel does not claim to have had such an experience himself, his mystical impulses surface quite clearly in his discussions of *teshuvah*.

Even if a person merely "thinks in his heart" of performing *teshuvah*, Yechiel maintains, the latent spiritual power of *teshuvah* itself instantaneously ascends heavenward. The mere *inclination* to repent/return serves as a catalyst for the elevation of spiritual desires. Its power is immediate and everlasting, and its scope immense. *Teshuvah* reaches not just the first or second levels of heaven but the highest heaven, God's very throne. Since it is beyond time and above space, *teshuvah* is truly a virtue of the spirit.

As a spiritual virtue, *teshuvah* holds considerable power. One of its greatest benefits to the *ba'al teshuvah*—the Jew "who has repented/returned"—is its ability not only to counteract but to *nullify* prior moral transgressions. Even the person who has performed evil acts every day of his or her life has the potential to regain moral footing through *teshuvah*. This virtue serves as a kind of spiritual broom, sweeping away all previous wrongdoing from the Jew's moral slate. Jews traditionally recite a "confession"—*vidui*—on two key occasions: Yom Kippur and their deathbeds. Whether the act of *teshuvah* is used to wipe out the sins of the past year or the sins of a lifetime, it is a very powerful tool indeed.

How is it possible for someone to become a *ba'al teshuvah*, to "return" to God? The first stage of transformation lies in consciousness. The potential *ba'al teshuvah* must gain awareness that he or she has sinned and must understand the shamefulness that results from those sins. The second stage is the battle to overcome the *yetzer hara*—"evil impulse." This is the struggle between the body and the soul, the conflict between wanting to do what feels good and the inner inclination to do what is right.

The outcome of this spiritual battle will determine whether or not one has become a true *ba'al teshuvah*. Yechiel offers the following strategy for victory: Since the ultimate price for moral transgression is exclusion from *Olam Haba*—the "World to Come"—the potential *ba'al teshuvah* should imagine the fleeting pleasure that he or she is about to experience and then contrast it with the pain of spiritual exile from the supreme and eternal pleasure of *Olam Haba*. When the stakes of this struggle become clear—temporary thrill versus everlasting joy—the *ba'al teshuvah* candidate will realize that there is only one proper path to follow.

It is only after defeating the evil impulse that a Jew can stand with fear and humility before God and consider himself or herself one who has been spiritually transformed. Contrition for one's sins, resolve never again to repeat them, and request for divine pardon all indicate that a person has reached the level of authentic *teshuvah*. The *ba'al teshuvah* will also come to understand that just as God forgives and negates the penitent's prior sins, God will punish the sins of the unrepentant.

Teshuvah is medicine for the soul. The Jew who commits acts of iniquity and transgression has a sick soul and is in dire need of healing. Just as bandages and medications help heal an unhealthy body, so does *teshuvah* help heal the moral and spiritual fiber of the unhealthy soul. Yet *teshuvah* does more than just heal the soul. It also mends the damaged relationship between the sinner and God. Although God may "despise" the person who pursues material pleasures and the evil inclination, the *ba'al teshuvah* will become one of the Holy One's most "beloved" and precious creations.

The pursuit of *teshuvah* must always be at the forefront of a Jew's body, mind, and soul. When we approach the gates of *teshuvah*, we must do so with heartfelt contrition, "with crying and with tears." We should follow our impulse toward *teshuvah* with as much fervor and passion as we follow our impulse toward bodily gratification. God opens a door for the penitent. Any human action that hinders or prevents *teshuvah* is *itself* a sin.

TESHUVAH IN JEWISH PIETISM

In contrast to the more philosophical works of other medieval religious thinkers, Bachya ibn Pakuda's treatise *Hovot ha-Levavot*, "Duties of the Heart," is concerned not so much with the rules of logic or absolute truth as with the *inner duties*, the spiritual and ethical principles that should guide our lives.

It is through the synthesis of the mind and the heart that the fullest understanding of *teshuvah* becomes possible. Bachya offers a definition. *Teshuvah*, he writes, means that

> a man fits himself to resume the service of the blessed Creator, after having withdrawn from it and sinned, so that what he had lost of the service is restored to him, whether this loss was occasioned by his ignorance of God and of the modes of serving God, or happened because his evil inclination had overpowered his understanding, or resulted from neglect of the duties he owed to God, association with evil companions who enticed him to sin, or similar causes.[1]

Like Yechiel, Bachya also describes *teshuvah* in terms of relationship. This virtue represents the mechanism by which a divine-human relationship that has been damaged can be repaired. *Teshuvah* becomes necessary when a Jew sins and thereby withdraws himself or herself from the service—*avodah*—of the Holy One, which is the central purpose of Jewish life and the foundation of Jewish spirituality. There are many ways in which a Jew might withdraw from God: ignorance of God's will, submission to the evil impulse, negligence, association with evildoers, etc. All of these actions or inactions result in the separation of the Jew from God.

Teshuvah alone has the power to mend this damage, to bring together again that which has been divided by sin. For Bachya, *teshuvah* has three basic manifestations. The first—and least meritorious—kind of *teshuvah* occurs when a Jew repents because he or she has not found a way—i.e., lacks the opportunity or means—to repeat the transgression. When the opportunity to commit that sin presents itself again, the individual will commit it. It is only *after* sinning that he or she will feel shame and regret. Such a person, according to Bachya, "repents with his mouth and not with his heart, in speech only but not in reality."[2] In other words, that person's *inner* life is still one of sin, despite appearances to the contrary.

The second type of *teshuvah* is demonstrated by the person who repents "with his heart and by deed," the person who is able to resist the evil impulse through mental and spiritual discipline. But this kind of *teshuvah* is also problematic because the person's inner being is still at war with itself. That person's evil impulse is constantly trying to draw him or her away from divine service and toward sin. As a result, so much energy is expended on trying to control the evil impulse that none is left to serve God. Only the complete renunciation of sin, and not just temporary victories over its pull, merits divine forgiveness.

The third and most complete form of *teshuvah* occurs when an individual fulfills all of its preconditions: the triumph of understanding over lust, constant dialogue with one's conscience, fear of and humility before God, reflectiveness, divine reverence, regret about past sins, and the heartfelt plea for forgiveness. All of these "duties of the heart" are essential elements for the process of reaching the level of true *teshuvah*, and they must all be practiced until the end of one's days. Only then is the penitent truly worthy of salvation.

TESHUVAH IN JEWISH PHILOSOPHY

It is not surprising that Maimonides, the Rambam, presents a portrait of *teshuvah* that is highly rationalistic and at the same time accessible and practical. In a section titled "The Laws of Repentance" in his *Mishneh Torah*, the Rambam explains his conception of authentic *teshuvah*.

> Perfect repentance occurs when an opportunity presents itself to the offender for repeating the offense and he refrains from committing it because of his repentance and not out of fear or physical inability. If, however, one repents only in his old age, when he is no longer able to do what he used to do, his repentance, although not the best, will, nevertheless, do him some good. Even if a person transgressed all his life and repented on the day of his death and died during his repentance, all his sins are pardoned.[3]

The issue of repentance is presented here with a great deal of common sense, which is consonant with the fact that the *Mishneh Torah* was written as a practical code for Jewish behavior and belief. Perfect repentance, *teshuvah gemurah*, is a virtue that must be demonstrated, both to oneself and to others. And it has two prerequisites. First, the potential penitent must resist the temptation to repeat the original offense when a new opportunity to commit it surfaces, and second, the motivation to refrain from the sin must stem from repentance itself, not from fear or the inability to perform it again. Although the act of repentance may be publicly observable, its impetus is not. *Teshuvah gemurah* must spring from an interior source, motivated by authentic contrition rather than by external pressures, such as the fear of punishment or physical limitations.

Like Bachya, the Rambam recognizes that there are different levels of *teshuvah*. If a person does not repent until well into his or her old age, when that person lacks the physical vitality either to crave or to perform the sins of his or her youth, repentance will still be beneficial, even if it is not *teshuvah* of the most meritorious type. Furthermore, if a person has lived an entire lifetime of sin and does not repent until the day of his or her death, that act of repentance will still be accepted and the person's sins will all be forgiven. For the Rambam, the power of *teshuvah* is eclipsed only by the breadth of God's mercy.

Nor is the importance of repentance limited to outward acts, like deception or theft.

> Just as a man must repent of these, so he must scan and search his evil traits, repenting of anger, hatred, envy, scoffing, greed, vainglory, etc. One must repent of all these failings. They are worse than sinful acts. When a person is addicted to them, he finds it difficult to eliminate them.[4]

God's vision encompasses not only external behavior but also internal attitude and intention. God's jurisdiction, therefore, extends beyond just the behavioral life of human beings. It reaches into our innermost depths. We are responsible and will thus be held accountable for all of our sins, whether they be sins of the hand or sins of the heart. According to the Rambam, it is these latter invisible transgressions that are the gravest and the hardest to expunge from our psychological and ethical systems. Society will not punish us for being greedy or hateful. Our impetus for *teshuvah* from these sins must derive from some other source, which is the moral conscience that God has implanted in us all.

For the average person, the quest for *teshuvah* is a daunting one, but we must not despair. The Rambam urges us not to think that reaching the level of the *tzadikim*—the "righteous ones"—is unattainable because of our sins for which we want to repent. Rather, the *ba'al teshuvah* is loved by God as if he or she had never sinned. In the Rambam's view, the merit of the repentant sinner is *superior* to that of someone who has never sinned because the penitent person has to exert greater effort to suppress the evil impulse that the *tzadik* has somehow managed to transcend.

Teshuvah: A Case Study

A spiritual virtue that holds the power to erase the ill effects of past actions is a formidable weapon in our existential struggle with sin. Since *teshuvah* is always possible for a human being, even up until the moment of death, *hope* is never alien to the human condition. To deprive a person of the possibility of repentance is to deprive that person of hope, to relegate him or her to a state of hopelessness and despair. That is why Yechiel regards placing obstacles in someone's path toward *teshuvah* as a sin in itself.

THE NEIGHBOR

Ten years ago, Niko was convicted of armed robbery. He has spent the last decade of his life behind bars, serving his sentence to its completion. Through correspondence courses, Niko has also earned a law degree and now intends to begin work as a legal aid lawyer. He feels that he has paid the price for his crime—which he never denied committing—and has become a new and better man. He regrets his past actions and has resolved to become a good citizen and a productive member of society.

Andrea and Saul live next to the apartment into which Niko has just moved. Within days, rumors about Niko's past had spread throughout the neighborhood and had reached them. The couple is confounded. They consider themselves liberals who believe in rehabilitation, but they have a young child and worry about her safety. They also do not feel comfortable living next door to a convicted felon. A petition that urges his removal from the community has been circulating in the neighborhood and has now reached them. After all the neighbors sign the petition, it will be given to local officials.

— *SHOULD ANDREA AND SAUL SIGN THE PETITION?* —

Questions for Discussion

1. What are the key issues that Andrea and Saul must consider before reaching a decision?

2. In your opinion, should the couple's fears for the welfare of their child and themselves influence their decision? If so, to what extent?

3. Is it possible or even desirable to try to resolve the conflict in this kind of situation only through the use of reason? Do you think that there are some decisions in which nonrational factors should play a role?

4. There are many ways to block the path to *teshuvah*. What are some other, less overt ways that this community might use to obstruct Niko's quest for repentance?

5. Is it possible for human beings to determine whether or not *teshuvah* has taken place in another person? How?

6. Can we simply forget someone's past actions? Should we leave forgiveness/pardon to God, or should we strive to exercise it ourselves?

7. In more spiritually sensitive communities, members might try to help smooth the potential penitent's path to *teshuvah*. In what ways could this be done?

---

[1] *Hovot ha-Levavot*, vol. 2, p. 131
[2] Ibid., p. 135
[3] *Mishneh Torah*, Book 1, *Hilkhot Teshuvah*, 2:1
[4] Ibid., 7:3

Shalom
שָׁלוֹם

Come, my students, and I will instruct you in the virtue/merit of peace. Know, my students, that the virtue of peace [shalom] is among the most exalted. That is why shalom is one of the names of the Holy One. As it is written: "Then Gideon [after God reassured him prior to his battle with the Midianites] built an altar there to God and called it *Adonai Shalom*." [Judges 6:24] And in every place in which peace is found, the fear of God is also found. And wherever there is no *shalom*, the fear/awe of heaven is not found.... So great is *shalom* that even the heavenly creatures need *shalom*. As it is written: *Oseh shalom bimeromav*—"God makes peace in the high places." [Job 25:2] So great is peace that they conclude the Priestly Benediction with it. As it is written: "And may God grant you peace." [Numbers 6:26] So great is peace that they end the *tefilah* with it. As it is written: "May God give strength to the people. May God bless God's people with peace." [Psalms 29:11] And not only that, but on the day of Israel's redemption, the announcement will begin with *shalom*. As it is written: "How welcome on the mountains are the feet of the messenger heralding good fortune, announcing peace." [Isaiah 52:7]

My students, come and see how great is the power of peace, that even with regard to those who hate, the Holy One said: "Greet them with *shalom*." As it is written: "When you approach a town to attack it, you shall

בָּנַי, בֹּאוּ וַאֲלַמֶּדְכֶם מַעֲלַת הַשָּׁלוֹם. דְּעוּ בָנַי, כִּי מַעֲלַת הַשָּׁלוֹם הִיא מִן הַמַּעֲלוֹת הָרָמוֹת, שֶׁכֵּן הוּא אֶחָד מִשְּׁמוֹתָיו שֶׁל הַקָּדוֹשׁ-בָּרוּךְ-הוּא, כָּעִנְיָן שֶׁנֶּאֱמַר, וַיִּקְרָא-לוֹ יְיָ שָׁלוֹם. וּבְכָל מָקוֹם שֶׁהַשָּׁלוֹם מָצוּי, שָׁם יִרְאַת-שָׁמַיִם מְצוּיָה. וּבְכָל מָקוֹם שֶׁאֵין שָׁם שָׁלוֹם, אֵין יִרְאַת-שָׁמַיִם מְצוּיָה.... גָּדוֹל הַשָּׁלוֹם, שֶׁאֲפִילוּ הָעֶלְיוֹנִים צְרִיכִין שָׁלוֹם, שֶׁנֶּאֱמַר, עֹשֶׂה שָׁלוֹם בִּמְרוֹמָיו. גָּדוֹל הַשָּׁלוֹם, שֶׁחוֹתְמִין בּוֹ בְּבִרְכַּת כֹּהֲנִים, שֶׁנֶּאֱמַר, וְיָשֵׂם לְךָ שָׁלוֹם. גָּדוֹל הַשָּׁלוֹם, שֶׁחוֹתְמִין בְּסוֹף הַתְּפִלָּה בְּשָׁלוֹם, שֶׁנֶּאֱמַר, יְיָ עֹז לְעַמּוֹ יִתֵּן יְיָ יְבָרֵךְ אֶת-עַמּוֹ בַשָּׁלוֹם. וְלֹא עוֹד אֶלָּא, שֶׁבְּיוֹם נֶחָמַת יִשְׂרָאֵל, מִתְבַּשְּׂרִין תְּחִלָּה בְּשָׁלוֹם, שֶׁנֶּאֱמַר, מַה-נָּאווּ עַל-הֶהָרִים רַגְלֵי מְבַשֵּׂר מַשְׁמִיעַ שָׁלוֹם.

בָּנַי, בֹּאוּ וּרְאוּ כַּמָּה גָּדוֹל כֹּחַ הַשָּׁלוֹם, שֶׁאֲפִילוּ לְשׂוֹנְאִים, אָמַר הַקָּדוֹשׁ-בָּרוּךְ-הוּא, פִּתְחוּ לָהֶן בְּשָׁלוֹם, כָּעִנְיָן שֶׁנֶּאֱמַר, כִּי-תִקְרַב אֶל-עִיר לְהִלָּחֵם עָלֶיהָ וְקָרָאתָ אֵלֶיהָ לְשָׁלוֹם. וַאֲפִילוּ בַּזְּמַן הַזֶּה, אָמְרוּ חֲכָמֵינוּ זִכְרוֹנָם לִבְרָכָה, שׁוֹאֲלִין בִּשְׁלוֹם הַגּוֹיִם, מִפְּנֵי דַּרְכֵי שָׁלוֹם. אָמְרוּ עָלָיו עַל רַבָּן יוֹחָנָן בֶּן זַכַּאי, שֶׁלֹּא הִקְדִּימוֹ אָדָם שָׁלוֹם בָּעוֹלָם וַאֲפִילוּ גּוֹי בַּשּׁוּק. וְאָמְרוּ חֲכָמֵינוּ זִכְרוֹנָם לִבְרָכָה, הֱוֵי מַקְדִּים

offer it terms of peace." [Deuteronomy 20:10] And even in our own time [when there is little or no contact between Jew and non-Jew], the sages, of blessed memory, said: "It is permitted to inquire after the peace of the non-Jews for the sake of peaceful ways." [*Shevi'it* 4:3] It was said about Rabbi Yochanan ben Zakkai that no man was first to greet him with *shalom*, not even a non-Jew in the marketplace, because he always greeted people first. And the sages, of blessed memory, said: "Greet every person with *shalom*, and be a tail to the lions rather than a head to the jackals." [*Pirkei Avot* 4:15]

בִּשְׁלוֹם כָּל אָדָם, וֶהֱוֵי זָנָב לָאֲרָיוֹת, וְאַל תְּהִי רֹאשׁ לַשּׁוּעָלִים.

…And what is the pursuit of peace? This is what the sages, of blessed memory, said: "The one who speaks of peace during a time of controversy and negates his own honor because of the group, just as Moses did. As it is written: "And Moses got up and went to Dathan and Abiram." [Numbers 16:25] And the one who gives up other business to help bring *shalom* between a husband and a wife, between friends, between a teacher and student. And even if one only prepares a meal for them, in order to make peace between them.

…וְאֵי זוֹ הִיא רְדִיפַת שָׁלוֹם? כָּךְ אָמְרוּ חֲכָמֵינוּ זִכְרוֹנָם לִבְרָכָה, זֶה הַמְדַבֵּר שָׁלוֹם בִּשְׁעַת מַחֲלֹקֶת, וּמְבַטֵּל כְּבוֹדוֹ מִפְּנֵי הָרַבִּים כְּדֶרֶךְ שֶׁעָשָׂה מֹשֶׁה, שֶׁנֶּאֱמַר, וַיָּקָם מֹשֶׁה וַיֵּלֶךְ אֶל־דָּתָן וַאֲבִירָם וְגוֹ׳. וְהַמְבַטֵּל עֲסָקָיו וּמַטִּיל שָׁלוֹם בֵּין אִישׁ לְאִשְׁתּוֹ, בֵּין אָדָם לַחֲבֵרוֹ, בֵּין רַב לְתַלְמִידוֹ. וַאֲפִילוּ הוּא עוֹשֶׂה סְעוּדָה לִשְׁנֵיהֶן, כְּדֵי לַעֲשׂוֹת שָׁלוֹם בֵּינֵיהֶן.

So great is peace that it even precedes the praise of God. For we find that when Jethro came to Moses, immediately each asked after the other's welfare and only then did Moses tell his father-in-law about all the miracles the Holy One had done on behalf of Israel. [Exodus 18:7-8] And not only that, but all the *mitzvot* that the wicked ones do in this world, the Holy One rewards them in this

גָּדוֹל הַשָּׁלוֹם שֶׁהוּא קוֹדֵם לְשִׁבְחוֹ שֶׁל מָקוֹם, שֶׁכֵּן כְּשֶׁבָּא יִתְרוֹ אֵצֶל מֹשֶׁה, מִיָּד וַיִּשְׁאֲלוּ אִישׁ־לְרֵעֵהוּ לְשָׁלוֹם, וְאַחַר־כָּךְ וַיְסַפֵּר מֹשֶׁה לְחֹתְנוֹ אֵת כָּל הַנִּסִּים שֶׁעָשָׂה [הַקָּדוֹשׁ־בָּרוּךְ־הוּא] לְיִשְׂרָאֵל. וְלֹא עוֹד אֶלָּא שֶׁכָּל הַמִּצְוֹת שֶׁעוֹשִׂין הָרְשָׁעִים בָּעוֹלָם הַזֶּה, הַקָּדוֹשׁ־בָּרוּךְ־הוּא נוֹתֵן שְׂכָרָן בָּעוֹלָם הַזֶּה, כְּגוֹן עֹשֶׁר וְחַיִּים

76

world with wealth, life, possessions, offspring, honor, and other good things—except for *shalom*, which the Holy One does not give them.

וּנְכָסִים וּבָנִים וְכָבוֹד וּשְׁאָר הַטּוֹבוֹת, חוּץ מִשָּׁלוֹם שֶׁאֵינוֹ נוֹתֵן לָהֶן.

[One of the opposites of *shalom*—"peace"—is *machaloket*—"controversy."]

My students, guard yourselves from controversy. One who stays away from it is honored by all…. And the sages, of blessed memory, said: "If there is unresolved controversy within a house, the house will end up being destroyed; in a synagogue, the synagogue will in the end break up/disperse; in a city, blood will spill in the city. Two sages who live in the same city or two courts with a standing controversy between them, in the end both will perish. And not only that, but controversy within a court of law brings destruction to the world. Know that it is true that whenever there is peace in the earthly assembly, there is peace in the heavenly assembly."

בָּנַי, תִּשְׁמְרוּ עַצְמְכֶם מִן הַמַּחֲלֹקֶת. שֶׁכָּל מִי שֶׁיּוֹשֵׁב לוֹ מִן הַמַּחֲלֹקֶת, הֲרֵי זֶה מְכֻבָּד בִּפְנֵי הַבְּרִיּוֹת…. וְאָמְרוּ חֲכָמֵינוּ זִכְרוֹנָם לִבְרָכָה, מַחֲלֹקֶת בַּבַּיִת, סוֹפוֹ לֶחָרֵב. מַחֲלֹקֶת בְּבֵית־הַכְּנֶסֶת, סוֹפוֹ לְהִתְפַּזֵּר. וְלֹא עוֹד אֶלָּא שֶׁסּוֹפוֹ לְהִשָּׁמֵם. מַחֲלֹקֶת בָּעִיר, שְׁפִיכוּת־דָּמִים בָּעִיר. שְׁנֵי תַּלְמִידֵי־חֲכָמִים הַדָּרִין בְּעִיר אַחַת וְכֵן שְׁנֵי בָתֵּי־דִינִין וּבֵינֵיהֶן מַחֲלֹקֶת, סוֹפָן לָמוּת. וְלֹא עוֹד אֶלָּא, שֶׁמַּחֲלֹקֶת בֵּית־דִּין, חָרְבַּן־עוֹלָם. תֵּדַע שֶׁכֵּן, שֶׁכָּל זְמַן שֶׁיֵּשׁ שָׁלוֹם בִּפָמַלְיָא שֶׁל מַטָּה, יֵשׁ שָׁלוֹם בִּפָמַלְיָא שֶׁל מַעְלָה.

[Another of the opposites of *shalom* is *leshon hara*—"slander, gossip."]

My students, if you see people seeking out defects in others and speaking about them, consider them to be evil people and slanderers and people who have a defect. As the sages said: "One person spoke of another in the presence of one of the great men. The great one said to him: 'You have told me about all your own defects while you are telling me so much about the defects of others. For the one who seeks a particular

בָּנַי, אִם רְאִיתֶם בְּנֵי־אָדָם מְחַזְּרִים וּמְחַפְּשִׂים אַחַר מוּמֵי בְּנֵי־אָדָם וּמְדַבְּרִים עֲלֵיהֶם, תַּחֲזִיקוּ אוֹתָם בְּחֶזְקַת רְשָׁעִים וּבַעֲלֵי לָשׁוֹן־הָרָע וּבַעֲלֵי־מוּמִין. כְּמוֹ שֶׁאָמְרוּ הַחֲכָמִים, שֶׁאָדָם אֶחָד דִּבֵּר בְּאָדָם אַחֵר אֵצֶל אֶחָד מִן הַגְּדוֹלִים. אָמַר לוֹ, הוֹדַעְתַּנִי עַל רֹב מוּמֶיךָ בְּמֶה שֶׁאַתָּה מַרְבֶּה לְסַפֵּר בְּמוּמֵי בְּנֵי־אָדָם. כִּי מְחַפֵּשׂ הַמּוּם, אֵינֶנּוּ מְחַפֵּשׂ אֶלָּא כְּפִי אֲשֶׁר בּוֹ מִמֶּנּוּ.

77

defect in others only looks for that which is defective in himself.'"

Woe to the gossipers, for they bring three punishments to the world: controversy, idol worship, and exile.

אוֹי לָהֶם לִמְסַפְּרֵי לָשׁוֹן־הָרָע, שֶׁהֵן מְבִיאִין שָׁלשׁ פֻּרְעָנִיּוֹת לָעוֹלָם. וְאֵלּוּ הֵן, מַחֲלֹקֶת, וַעֲבוֹדָה־זָרָה, וְגָלוּת.

And whoever is regularly involved with peace and loves and pursues peace and tries to establish *shalom* between a husband and a wife and between friends, the Holy One spreads the shelter of peace over that kind of person, measure for measure. As it is written: "O God, arrange peace for us because all of our actions You do for us." [Isaiah 26:12]

And whoever loves and pursues peace merits and will witness the coming of the Messiah, for that will mark the beginning of *shalom*. As it is written: "How welcome on the mountain are the feet of the messenger heralding good fortune, announcing peace." [Isaiah 52:7] And Isaiah also says: "Behold, I will extend peace to her [Jerusalem] like a river. [Isaiah 66:12]

וְכָל מִי שֶׁרָגִיל בְּשָׁלוֹם וְאוֹהֵב שָׁלוֹם וְרוֹדֵף שָׁלוֹם וּמֵשִׂים שָׁלוֹם בֵּין אִישׁ לְאִשְׁתּוֹ וּבֵין אָדָם לַחֲבֵרוֹ, הַקָּדוֹשׁ־בָּרוּךְ־הוּא פּוֹרֵשׂ עָלָיו סֻכַּת שְׁלוֹמוֹ, מִדָּה כְּנֶגֶד מִדָּה, כָּעִנְיָן שֶׁנֶּאֱמַר, יְיָ תִּשְׁפֹּת שָׁלוֹם לָנוּ כִּי גַם כָּל־מַעֲשֵׂינוּ פָּעַלְתָּ לָנוּ.

וְכָל מִי שֶׁאוֹהֵב שָׁלוֹם וְרוֹדֵף שָׁלוֹם, זוֹכֶה וְרוֹאֶה בְּבִיאַת מָשִׁיחַ, שֶׁבִּשְׁעַת בִּיאָתוֹ פּוֹתֵחַ תְּחִלָּה בְּשָׁלוֹם, כָּעִנְיָן שֶׁנֶּאֱמַר, מַה־נָּאווּ עַל־הֶהָרִים רַגְלֵי מְבַשֵּׂר מַשְׁמִיעַ שָׁלוֹם. וְכֵן הוּא אוֹמֵר, הִנְנִי נוֹטֶה־אֵלֶיהָ כְּנָהָר שָׁלוֹם.

Commentary

Anyone who has ever read Jewish liturgy knows that the word *shalom*—"peace"—is central to the rabbinic worldview. The Jew prays for peace perhaps more than for anything else, sometimes in reference to a real situation, sometimes as an expression of hope for the future. But no matter the context in which the word *shalom* is used, it quickly becomes apparent that *shalom* means far more than merely the absence of strife and conflict. Yechiel begins his discussion of *shalom* not in the sociopolitical realm but in the spiritual one.

Yechiel claims that *shalom* is intimately connected to God and that it is more than just an attribute. *Shalom* is one of God's names. Peace is not only a quality that God expresses, like compassion or forgiveness, but a description of who God *is*. In this way, *shalom* is as much connected to holiness as it is to behavior or to a state of affairs. Perhaps that is why Yechiel notes that wherever *boshet* or *shalom* is found, the fear of God will also be present.

As a virtue connected to holiness, *shalom* plays a role both in heaven and on earth. It has celestial as well as terrestrial dimensions. Just as God makes peace here on earth, so does God make peace in the heavens. (This implies that the heavens, too, suffer from discord and disharmony.) The *Birkat Kohanim*—"Priestly Benediction"—closes with a prayer for peace. So does the final blessing of the *Amidah*. Peace, it seems, serves as a kind of punctuation mark in Jewish liturgy. It is the greatest wish expressed by a Jew in his or her dialogue with God. These messianic undertones reach full flower in Isaiah, where we learn that *shalom* will not only accompany Israel's redemption but will be its very harbinger.

The wish for peace, however, must not be limited to certain individuals or groups. We must offer *shalom* even to those we hate. The most loathsome of characters, those whom we view as our mortal enemies, are still deserving, at least initially, of an offer of peace. And the Jewish virtue of *shalom* should not be restricted to Jews alone. Our focus must be messianic in nature: *Shalom* must not be moored in particularism. For the sake of "peaceful ways," a Jew ought to be concerned with the welfare of non-Jews in his or her community as well as that of Jews.

What does being a *rodef shalom*—a "pursuer of peace"—mean? The Jew who pursues peace is a person who is willing to take risks, to go against public opinion, even to jeopardize his or her own position within the community in order to bring about *shalom*. In a time of conflict, when those around us are ready to wage war over this or that cause, the *rodef shalom* will speak in favor of peaceful resolution. Advocating such an unpopular view may cause a person to lose face with his or her neighbors and friends. But the *rodef shalom*, whose basic principle is the pursuit of peace, is willing to suspend or even sacrifice his or her own social standing or obligations in order to make peace between others.

According to Yechiel, the pursuit of peace is so great a virtue that it precedes even the praise of God. When one must choose between praying and making peace, the latter has priority. But *shalom* is not only a goal; it is also a reward. God will grant peace to the righteous but withhold it from the wicked. As a result, although the wicked may gain material benefits from whatever good deeds they might perform (in addition to their crimes), they will never find the psychospiritual gift of peace. Whether they are pursued by the forces of goodness or their own inner demons, the wicked will never find rest in this world.

One of the opposites of *shalom* is *machaloket*—"conflict." This is a situation that the Jew must strive to avoid. It is destructive to all interpersonal relationships, from the smallest to the greatest. Whether the *machaloket* occurs in a household, a synagogue, or a city, it will eventually break up and destroy that structure if it is left unresolved. Conflict tears apart our world. For there to be peace in the heavens, for the world to reach a state of harmony, there must first be peace among human beings.

Another opposite of the virtue of *shalom* is *leshon hara*—"slander." To speak against someone is to seek "defects" in that person, to try to tear him or her down. When we find someone engaged in *leshon hara*—be it simple gossip or outright defamation—we must confront that individual in the same way that we would confront a wicked person. Rather than listening to a person's criticism of someone else, we must force that individual to face his or her *own* faults and imperfections. We are taught to do this because a person who speaks *leshon hara*, who actively seeks out weaknesses in others, does so in response to those weaknesses that reside within himself or herself. By tearing down others, such a person puts himself or herself on a pedestal.

Although the pursuit of peace is a selfless endeavor at its core, the *rodef shalom* will reap some significant rewards from it. The first reward is the gift of peace. In trying to establish peace where there is strife (e.g., between husband and wife, between friends), the *rodef shalom* will motivate God to spread "the shelter of peace" over him or her as well. The second reward is messianic in nature. Whoever loves and pursues peace will not only merit but will also personally "witness" the coming of the Messiah. Since peace will be the harbinger of the End of Days, it follows that the one who pursues the path of peace will find, just a bit farther along the way, the road to redemption.

SHALOM IN JEWISH PHILOSOPHY

Moses Maimonides, who was introduced in Chapter 1, deals extensively with the concept of *shalom* but does so in less explicit ways than Yechiel. Maimonides, known as the Rambam, lived during the social and political turmoil of the Middle Ages. He viewed peace largely as the absence of conflict and strife. As a result, even his theological writings on the topic have sociopolitical hues.

Like Yechiel, the Rambam connects the concept of peace with the Messianic Age. The Rambam argues that "great evils," like hatred, violence, and war, stem not from sinfulness but from ignorance, the privation of knowledge. Only after these evils are obliterated will the time of the Messiah—the time of peace—be at hand.

> Just as a blind man, because of absence of sight, does not cease stumbling...because he has nobody to guide him on his way, the various sects of men—every individual according to the extent of his ignorance—do to themselves and to others great evils.... If there were knowledge, whose relation to the human form is like that of the faculty of sight to the eye, they would refrain from doing any harm to

themselves and to others. For through cognition of the truth, enmity and hatred are removed and the inflicting of harm by people on one another is abolished. It holds out this promise, saying, "And the wolf shall dwell with the lamb, and the leopard shall lie down with the kid." (Isaiah 11:6)[1]

The acquisition of knowledge is like the acquisition of sight: It will prevent moral "stumbling" and seems to support Plato's claim that "to know the good is to do the good." For the Rambam, the messianic vision of peace and harmony is viewed as the result of the triumph of the intellect over humanity's more destructive impulses. All of the evils that produce strife and disharmony spring from ignorance, from the failure to discover and actualize the power of our reason. The apprehension of truth, which the Rambam also calls "the knowledge of God," will eliminate those irrational elements that lead to all forms of interpersonal conflict and violence.

The Rambam argues that the Jewish conception of the End Time is not a period of Israel's conquest over the nations, as it is in many midrashic legends about the Apocalypse. Nor is it a time of eating, drinking, and celebrating, as it is in other traditions. Far from being a time of material pursuits and pleasures, the Messianic Age will be a time for peace and *intellectual* perfection, an era in which Israel will "be free to study Torah, with no one to oppress or disturb them."[2]

In this context, the pursuit of peace and the pursuit of knowledge coalesce. Knowledge will lead to peace, and peace will lead to yet more knowledge. In the Messianic Era

> there will be no famine, no war, no envy, no strife…. The universal preoccupation will be primarily to know God…. The things that are now vague and deeply hidden will be revealed to all; they will attain a knowledge of their Creator to the utmost human capacity. As it is written: "The land shall be full of the knowledge of God, as the waters cover the sea." (Isaiah 11:9)[3]

When natural and moral evils no longer exist, when strife and bloodshed are replaced with peace and harmony, when truth and the knowledge of God become the activity and the property of all people, then and only then will we find ourselves in a world and in a time that can fittingly be called messianic.

SHALOM IN JEWISH THOUGHT

The Maharal of Prague removes the concept of *shalom* from its sociopolitical and intellectual context and places it squarely in the domain of the spiritual. In order to help us grasp the Maharal's approach to this topic, we should note that the word for peace, *shalom*, comes from a root that is related to completeness. According to the Maharal, absolute completeness— *shelemut*—is nothing less than *shalom* in its most perfect form, the ultimate realization of peace.

Like Yechiel, the Maharal claims that *shalom* is a name for God. He implies that peace is an integral element of God's essence and nature and a foundation for the very existence of the world and its inhabitants. He writes:

> God makes peace between all that exists. If God did not make peace
> between the opposites [that also exist] in the world, the world could
> not stand.... God embraces all with *shalom*, for God is the ultimate
> form of the world and thereby makes everything whole.... Since God
> is the ultimate form of the world, God embraces all and connects and
> unifies all—and this is the very essence of peace.[4]

One of God's most critical functions, the Maharal maintains, is that of *unification*. Without God's unifying power, everything that exists would be in a state of perpetual and irreconcilable tension. Hot and cold could never become warm; fire and water could never become steam; day and night could never become dusk or dawn. Even the most basic acts, like inhaling and exhaling air, would become impossible. In short, the world and all life forms within it would end.

Peace is the force that unites all opposites and makes a single totality out of diverse and conflicting parts. *Shalom* is the principle that reconciles, harmonizes, and neutralizes the poles of existence. Yet *shalom* is about more than just the physical. Since God is the "ultimate form" of the world—a form that is spiritual, not material, in its essence—the quality of peace represents divine perfection, that state of *shelemut* that has actualized every potential and as yet unrealized nature. Peace is the sum total of all that exists, and only God is capable of embracing all. As the Maharal writes, "God alone constitutes the essence of peace."[5]

Shalom: A Case Study

According to Yechiel, a Jew for whom the pursuit of peace is the highest of objectives is a *rodef shalom*, a model of virtue not just for the community of Israel but also for the world. The *rodef shalom* is concerned with doing what is right and good and not with his or her own status or position within the community. The *rodef shalom* is willing to take risks and make an extra effort in order to bring about peaceful resolutions to life's conflicts.

BEYOND THE CALL OF DUTY

Dan has been Hector's good friend for many years. When Hector married his wife, Joyce, Dan became close to her as well. The first few years of Hector and Joyce's marriage were wonderful, but lately the two of them argue about everything. They are about to get a divorce. Dan thinks that a divorce would be a tragic mistake for them and for their two children. He believes that their problems are surmountable and that they should work through their differences for their own sake and for that of their family.

Dan has devoted much time trying to help his two friends. Both Hector and Joyce are very depressed. Dan desperately wants to make peace between them. He has offered to take the children for a weekend so that Hector and Joyce could be alone and try to sort things out. He has given them the names and telephone numbers of several marriage counselors in their area. He has met with them together and on an individual basis and has listened to them vent their frustrations. But Hector and Joyce have just told Dan that they no longer want his help or anybody else's. They simply want to be left alone.

——————— WHAT SHOULD DAN DO? ———————

QUESTIONS FOR DISCUSSION

1. Should Dan continue trying to help his friends or should he observe their wishes? Why?

2. How much of Dan's motivation seems to be "pure" altruism (the desire to help others)? What interest might *he* have in the outcome of this situation?

3. Is it possible for someone to benefit from good things that happen to someone else? If so, in what ways? Does the benefit the person receives detract from the moral worth of his or her motivation?

4. Is Dan a *rodef shalom* in this context? Explain.

5. What consequences might Dan face if he continues on this course of action? Are they worth it?

6. If spending time with Hector and Joyce begins to affect Dan's own family life, should he stop? At what point must he make that decision? Why?

7. When does selflessness become intrusiveness? How far is *too* far?

---

[1] *The Guide for the Perplexed* (Chicago, 1963), pp. 440-441
[2] *Mishneh Torah*, Book 14, *Hilkhot Melakhim*, 12:4
[3] Ibid., 12:5
[4] *Netivot Olam*, vol. 1, 8:1
[5] Ibid.